THE FINANCIAL
SERVICES
MARKETING
HANDBOOK

THE FINANCIAL SERVICES MARKETING HANDBOOK

Tactics and Techniques That Produce Results

Second Edition

Evelyn Ehrlich and Duke Fanelli

BLOOMBERG PRESS
An Imprint of
WILEY

Published by John Wiley & Sons, Inc., Hoboken, New Jersey.
Published simultaneously in Canada.

For general information on our other products and services or for technical support, please contact our Customer Care Department within the United States at (800) 762-2974, outside the United States at (317) 572-3993, or fax (317) 572-4002.

Wiley also publishes its books in a variety of electronic formats. Some content that appears in print may not be available in electronic books. For more information about Wiley products, visit our web site at www.wiley.com.

Library of Congress Cataloging-in-Publication Data:

Ehrlich, Evelyn, 1950–
    The financial services marketing handbook : tactics and techniques that produce results / Evelyn Ehrlich and Duke Fanelli. — 2nd ed.
        p.   cm.
    Includes bibliographical references and index.
    ISBN 978-1-118-06571-6 (cloth); ISBN 978-1-118-25570-4 (ebk);
    ISBN 978-1-118-23636-9 (ebk); ISBN 978-1-118-22240-9 (ebk)
        1. Financial services industry—United States—Marketing.   2. Financial planners—Marketing.
3. Customer relations.   4. Financial services industry—Computer network resources.   I. Fanelli, Duke, 1954– II. Title.
    HG181.E38   2012
    332.1068'8—dc23   2011041422

Printed in the United States of America

10 9 8 7 6 5 4 3 2 1

Contents

SECTION TWO: MARKETING TACTICS

Preface

When we wrote the first edition of *The Financial Services Marketing Handbook*, our goal was to help codify financial marketing theory and practice as a training tool for both students and practitioners. We have been gratified by the response to the first edition, published in 2004 by Bloomberg Press: It has been adopted as a course text in undergraduate and graduate programs at major universities; distributed in bulk as a training tool for corporate programs; well-reviewed in the trade press; used for presentations at national and international financial conferences; and translated into various languages, including Chinese and Indonesian.

A lot has changed since the first edition was published in 2004. For one, many of the companies cited as examples in the earlier edition no longer exist. The names of the fallen are, in some respects, a history of the 2008 financial crisis: Bear Stearns, Lehman Brothers, Countrywide, Washington Mutual, Wachovia. Some of these firms (Washington Mutual, Wachovia among them) were marketing leaders whose marketing savvy couldn't overcome bad business practices. It was not the lack of marketing awareness that caused the financial crash of 2008—if anything, some of these companies were too good at marketing bad securities. But the state of financial marketing has become more difficult with the crisis—there is less trust in financial institutions and more defections from long-standing relationships. Marketers cannot manufacture trust. It inheres to the product or service and grows from a company-wide commitment to serving customer needs.

In addition to the impact of the crisis on many financial brands, another major change has occurred in the last decade in the tools of marketing. When the first edition came out, the Internet was only a few years old and many practitioners viewed online marketing as an optional, rather than a core, practice. Today, online media are integral to any marketing campaign and are, therefore, integrated into the chapters on various tactical approaches—from public relations to face-to-face selling, from advertising to event sponsorship. We have added a sub-chapter on mobile and smartphone marketing and created a new chapter focusing specifically on the social media—blogging, social networks, and other modalities sometimes referred to as Web 2.0. This chapter may date just as rapidly as the earlier Internet chapter it replaced. Web 3.0 and 4.0 are in the wings and financial marketers will need to figure out how to harness these tools, while coming to grips with a new paradigm in which we no longer control the conversation but rather respond to what the market says.

In a way, though, the rise of the social web takes marketers back to first principles: Listen to customers, learn what their needs are, respond with products and services that meet those needs. The basic principles of marketing have not changed. Segmentation, positioning and strategic planning are more important than ever. Financial marketers have to do more with less and need more than ever to prioritize strategic and tactical goals and measure results. "Seat of the pants" marketing continues to be the default mode for many financial companies but if the last decade has taught us anything, it is that bad marketing decisions have serious consequences.

Our hope is that this new edition of *The Financial Services Marketing Handbook* will help financial marketers make better decisions by reviewing core principles and learning from the successes and failures of others.

Evelyn Ehrlich
Duke Fanelli
March 2012

Acknowledgments

Many people helped us by giving their time, knowledge, and support: We would especially like to thank Renee Harris of New York University's Center for Marketing; Bill Wreaks; the editor of the first edition, Jared Kieling; Laura Walsh and Judy Howarth at Wiley; and all our colleagues and clients who have educated and supported us over the course of our (collective) 50 years in financial services marketing.

Duke Fanelli co-authored this book based on a desire to share, demystify, and make useful the many tools at the disposal of the financial services marketer and practitioner. His contributions to this book would not have been possible without his wife Donna's unyielding support, enthusiasm, and encouragement for all his life's endeavors, and his children Michael, Carina, and Alicia who provide daily inspiration. Special thanks go to the ANA (Association of National Advertisers), which made its collective marketing knowledge and deep insights available.

Evelyn Ehrlich would like to dedicate this book in loving memory of her parents, Liesel and Fritz Ehrlich.

The Unique Challenges of Marketing Financial Services

Marketing financial services used to be easier. Banks gave a toaster to a new depositor and had a customer for life. Stockbrokers rarely left their parent company to go to a competitor. Institutional financial services was a clubby business in which multimillion-dollar deals were negotiated on the golf course. No more. Today, competition in financial services is fierce; sales and market-share growth can hinge on a few basis points, a friendlier voice on the phone, or an easier-to-navigate web site. Not only has competition become more intense, financial services have also changed structurally. Old customs and laws that isolated banks by geography and separated investment banks from commercial banks, and insurance companies from mutual fund companies, have disappeared.

Now, everyone is competing for hot business segments. Retirement services, for example, are offered by banks, brokerages, mutual funds, insurance companies, and independent advisers. And it's not just customers they're competing for. With mergers and acquisitions occurring all the time, financial companies are no longer lifelong employers to whom employees naturally feel loyalty. Today's financial marketplace is a free for all, where top sales producers act like pro basketball players, demanding signing bonuses and salaries that can far exceed the CEO's.

But even as the financial industry has undergone momentous structural change, financial services marketing has remained pretty much what it's always been: passive, conservative, and relatively undisciplined. The words are different now; marketing managers talk about "brand management" and "customer value" and "share of wallet." But with few exceptions, financial services marketers are using old and not always effective methods of acquiring and retaining customers and sales professionals. This is true both in consumer and institutional markets, in traditional brick-and-mortar businesses like banks, and in cutting-edge businesses like online brokerages.

Some financial companies have attempted to update their methods by applying lessons learned in more marketing-oriented disciplines, such as consumer products. And there are certainly lessons to be learned that way. One of the objectives of this

1

book is to introduce and apply modern marketing principles to the practice of financial marketing.

But financial products are not consumer products. In fact, they're not products at all in the way product marketing is usually described. Nor are they altogether like services.

The financial industry operates in a unique way, and its marketing tasks are correspondingly complex. Consider an example: Product marketers can target consumers and can position and brand their products with the confidence that all samples of their products are manufactured to be the same—every bottle of Stolichnaya vodka tastes the same, looks the same. But a marketing manager at a private bank can't make the same assumption. The experience that clients have of the bank's service will differ, depending on the particular private banker who serves them and on support staff throughout the organization.

If financial products don't act like products, neither do they act entirely like services. Consider that, in many cases, a "product" will be sold not by someone who works for the parent company but by someone who is independent—an insurance broker, pension fund adviser, or personal financial planner. Or they may work for the parent company but still act independently, as do many stockbrokers who can easily walk away to a new firm. Your job as a marketer is not only to make sure that sales professionals are sustaining your brand strategy but also to keep them selling your product. You've got a two-tiered marketing task: Selling the customer and selling the salesperson.

And this only begins to describe the challenges for the financial services marketer. Even defining financial services is hard in an industry that encompasses everything from mass-marketing of consumer banking, insurance, and investments to one-on-one selling of institutional products and services that may cost millions of dollars.

This book is designed for anyone whose job it is to market or sell any financial product or service—consumer or institutional—through a multitude of sales channels. The following chapters provide the basic tools and techniques that every financial marketer needs to be familiar with, along with case studies of how these methods have been applied (some successfully, some less so). To begin, let's look more closely at how financial marketing is different.

Products or Services?

In order to apply general marketing principles to financial services, we first need to ask: Are the goods being sold as products or as services? What difference does it make? For your bottom line, plenty. Let's say, for example, that you're in charge of a new credit card, called Topnotch, for the high-net-worth market. It offers lots of extras and has a hefty annual fee. One of your jobs, as a product marketer, would be to use focus groups, surveys, and other market-research methods in order to help the product people determine which bells and whistles would be most valued by prospective

Advertising Is Not Marketing

We've run into a lot of people, often in sales, who think that the most essential thing you need in order to improve sales is advertising. Or conversely, we've run into other people, also often in sales, who don't believe in marketing because advertising doesn't work. So let's get this straight right away; advertising is only one tool in marketing, and it's not always a central one. Anyone who wants to increase business is going to look for the fastest and easiest way to do it, which usually means committing a lot of money. And yes, a good ad campaign can call attention to a crowded product category, as Grey New York demonstrated with its campaign for E*TRADE.

But marketing is a discipline that requires strategic thinking more than it requires a big budget. Careful planning means setting goals, choosing target market segments, determining or creating a product's differentiation and positioning, and selecting the tactics that will get the product noticed and bought by your targets. Successful marketing can mean playing golf with your best client's CEO, or it can mean opening new markets in Asia. What's important is not just what you do but why you do it.

The talking baby ads have been a big hit for E*TRADE since they debuted during the Super Bowl broadcast in 2008. One of many online trading firms that cropped up during the first dot-com fervor in the late 1990s, E*TRADE is among the few of its contemporaries still on the scene. One of the reasons for its longevity has been a willingness to break through the clutter by creating amusing advertising that has generated viral success—and added to the bottom line.

But note that the ads, while certainly attention-getting, also work on the level of matching the brand image with the firm's positioning strategy. The point of the campaign is that E*TRADE makes investing so easy that even a baby can do it. Other online brokerages could make the same claim—but the baby gets the message across with humor and charm—qualities not usually found in financial advertising.

Of course, as a direct-to-consumer marketer, E*TRADE has more room to maneuver than many financial firms. Smart advertising is only one of the tactics that marketers can use to support their overall goals. See Chapter 4 for a more detailed discussion of advertising and what makes it effective.

customers and how much they would be willing to pay for them. You would then need to pinpoint your product's advantages over your competition and find a way to communicate these benefits to your target market segment. This is all classic product marketing.

You've done all this brilliantly, and your Topnotch card has taken off beyond your projections. But then you start noticing some disturbing numbers—customers are canceling their cards far beyond the levels you anticipated. And after a lot of interviews with current and former customers, you find out that the service provided on your card is uneven. Sometimes the customer service representatives are extremely helpful, but other times they leave the customer unsatisfied. And the reason is that even though they are trained to offer Topnotch service, the reps' compensation is tied to the number of customers they service rather than the satisfaction of each customer they service. As a result, the customers' experience with the card does not match the brand image of luxury and customization. Your mistake was to market a product (all Topnotch cards are the same), rather than a service (each experience of using the Topnotch card is different).

Financial Services as Products

As the example shows, financial services are neither products nor services, but have elements of each. Here are some ways in which financial services are like products:

Separability. Unlike many services, the production of many financial products can be separated from their consumption. A consumer does not have to be physically present in the bank to use a checking account. Like an athletic shoe, the checking account is "manufactured" in advance of its sale and subsequent use.

Lack of perishability. Unlike a dinner reservation, a credit card will be there when the customer wants one. It is not perishable. This makes it easier for the financial provider to manage supply and demand. Unlike the finite seating in a restaurant where every customer wants a table on Saturday at 8 p.m., the supply of credit cards can be adjusted to meet demand.

Mass production. Services are typically created and delivered one at a time, while products are usually mass produced. Whereas many financial services are individualized, such as financial advice, others can be mass produced and mass marketed, like insurance policies, college savings accounts, or data-analysis systems for bond traders. Mass production enables mass distribution and cost savings.

Financial Services as Services

A checking account may be "manufactured," but it is not tangible. Unlike a car, you can't touch it or examine its features with your eyes and hands. It has no physical presence. Despite the vocabulary often employed in the financial world, financial services "products" are not entirely products, because they are intangible. Intangibles have certain common qualities.

Low cost of entry. There is little or no cost to manufacture, inventory, or distribute a financial "product." Start-up costs are very low, which means that there are few barriers to creating—or copying—a financial product. Although there may be legal restrictions and expenses associated with marketing, the capital costs of creating a new product are negligible. Also, there are no warehousing or physical distribution costs.

Speed to market. A manufacturer of a new toy or airplane must develop blueprints, build models, test the integrity of the design, and often reengineer several prototypes before a product can even be test-marketed. But in financial services, the idea is the product. If an investment bank comes up with a new way to securitize cash flow (say, by selling shares of the future royalties of a pop singer), the bank can start selling the securities almost as soon as the ink is dry on the offering plan.

Lack of exclusivity. A successful new manufactured product can usually enjoy a period of exclusivity, during which there is no competition. The product may be patented (like a drug) or trademarked (like software) to prevent competitors from using exactly the same formulation. Or the costs of building a competitive manufacturing facility (as for a new airplane model) are just too high to be feasible.

Nearly Anyone Can Start a Hedge Fund

From 2000 to 2008, the "hot" investing vehicle for institutions such as pension funds was the hedge fund. These lightly regulated investment funds are so named because of their ability to hedge their investments by buying options, futures, or otherwise protecting against downside risk—and oftentimes they far exceeded the return of the stock market.

Starting a new hedge fund requires not much more than a telephone and a computer. Hedge fund managers are active traders, which makes them highly profitable to Wall Street trading and clearing firms. As a result, large firms such as JPMorgan Chase and Morgan Stanley, along with many smaller firms, have prime brokerage programs that attempt to woo new hedge fund managers with a range of services. These may include providing office space, technology services, marketing support, initial advice on legal and accounting issues, and even start-up money and introductions to the brokerage firm's own clients. Thus, the amount of capital a new hedge fund manager has to raise up front can be very small indeed.

Not surprisingly, given the ease of entry and potentially huge fees, the number of hedge funds skyrocketed. In 2000, there were fewer than 3,000 hedge funds worldwide; by the market peak in 2007, there were more than 13,000 hedge funds.[1] With the market crash—and the disappointing performance of many of these funds—the total number and asset size of hedge funds began to decline.

But in financial services, there are few protections, and the cost of entry is low. Merrill Lynch "invented" the first CMA (cash management account) in the late 1970s. It was the first time that a brokerage firm had offered an account that combined investments with checking. It was very successful and brought Merrill a lot of new business. But within a few years, every brokerage firm had one. Although Merrill trademarked the name, it could not protect the idea. Its first-mover advantage quickly dissipated.

Service Is What It's About

Because it's easy to copy a new financial idea, product differentiation is difficult. Whatever bells and whistles you come up with for your product, for example, affiliation credit cards or Smartphone bank deposits, can be easily replicated by your competitors. Over time, additional value has to come from somewhere other than the product itself.

Where does added value come from? Service is almost always the most important differentiator. With products, you can control quality at the source—in the manufacturing process. With a service, quality is added (or not) by the people who sell to or manage the clients. This means that the quality of your product can vary because of the individual who is selling or providing it. All Verizon iPhones are the same, but all financial advisers are not. Thus, one of the biggest challenges within organizations that are marketing financial services is controlling service quality. This is particularly difficult in those areas where third parties who are not employed by the service creator are responsible for servicing your product—such as investment advisers, independent insurance agents, or third-party administrators of pension plans.

Psychology of Money

Financial services are about money, and money carries a lot of psychological baggage. People's attitudes toward money are highly emotional. This may matter less at the institutional level, but for the consumer marketer, hitting the right emotional notes can be critical. One financial institution, for example, developed a typology that classified attitudes and behaviors toward financial matters into five categories, based on the following variables: degree of control over spending and saving, interest in and knowledge about money matters, desire to accumulate versus spend, and trust in or need for advice.

Other typologies have addressed investor psychology—for example, market-follower versus contrarian, degree of risk tolerated, or spending and saving behaviors. Spending and saving typologies go back to Freud, who described compulsive spenders and non-spenders, as well as subtypes, such as the pretended wealthy and the pretended poor. Modern psychologists have built on Freudian taxonomies, describing categories such as "fanatical shoppers," "passive buyers," and "esteem buyers." Marketers of debt

---

Behavioral Economics

An entire discipline has emerged in recent years called "behavioral economics," which has become increasingly influential, particularly in the marketing of investments. The insights from this discipline have shown that, contrary to classical economic theory, humans do not behave rationally when it comes to investing.

For example, experiments have shown that an investment loss is at least twice as painful as a gain is pleasurable. This and other insights have begun to influence the way marketers craft their messages. For example, clients are more likely to say yes to a question asking if they would invest in a security that had an 80 percent chance of gain than a 20 percent chance of loss.[2] While all marketers benefit from the work of psychologists, only financial services marketers have a Nobel Prize-winning discipline to undergird their efforts.

---

products are particularly interested in the psychology of spending because they seek to identify targets who are likely to build up balances while continuing to pay them off steadily. There is a fine line between overspenders who default and those who do not.

Third-Party Relationships

Because money is so personal, relationships become very important in some areas of financial services—particularly investments, retirement planning, and insurance. Consumers don't necessarily buy a brand (Morgan Stanley) so much as they do an individual (my stockbroker). In fact, in some cases, the person who sells the product is also the creator of the product, for example, independent financial advisers. For the marketer, the fact that the customer has a relationship with a financial intermediary is a double-edged sword. On the one hand, customer loyalty tends to be very high. On the other hand, today's Morgan Stanley sales executive may be tomorrow's Merrill Lynch sales executive—and his or her clients will generally follow along. Thus, the marketer's task is as much to sell to the intermediary as it is to sell to the end user.

Multiple Sales Channels

One of the reasons for the complexity of marketing financial services is that there are numerous ways to reach the end customer. In conventional product marketing, you generally have a sales chain: manufacturer to wholesaler or distributor, to retail store, to customer. The sales reps for a pharmaceutical company are talking to doctors; for a consumer products company, to retailers. The end user is seldom the manufacturer's customer.

In financial services, end users are reached directly and indirectly, sometimes in both ways at the same time. Each sales channel requires a different marketing strategy. Here are some of the possible avenues:

Direct to end user. Methods include direct mail (often used by credit card companies), telemarketing, and online sales (online brokerage services, some loans and insurance products).

Commissioned salespeople. This is the most common way institutional products are sold, via employees or dedicated representatives of the manufacturer. The model is prevalent in retail services as well, for example, stockbrokers or insurance agents who are compensated by the company that creates the products, such as Merrill Lynch or State Farm.

Independent commissioned sales agents. Third-party sales to consumers are commonplace in the investment and insurance industries. In this arrangement, the financial adviser or insurance agent represents numerous lines of business. When the agents sell a product (such as a mutual fund) to the end consumer, they receive a commission from that mutual fund management company.

Independent noncommissioned advisers. Some advisers—including investment advisers, pension consultants, and insurance brokers—are paid by their customers to provide advice that is not influenced by commissions. Their job is to investigate the entire universe of products and select those that are most suitable for their customers.

Retail. Banks traditionally have relied on brick-and-mortar branches as their primary sales channel. Other companies that have physical branches include brokerage firms, mutual fund companies, and specialty providers, such as H&R Block.

How End Users Select a Financial Services Provider

When buying a tangible product, consumers can choose which product to buy on a comparative basis. Savvy customers will consider technical specifications (which computer has the fastest processor?), availability, reliability, warranties, and other items that can be assessed on an apples-to-apples basis. And, of course, they can compare prices. Financial services are rarely comparison-shopped this way. Although the Internet has made it easier to compare, say, mortgage rates or the price of term-life policies, decisions about financial providers are often based on factors beyond the marketer's control. For example, convenience—the closest bank branch, the credit card solicitation that arrived today—will often trump better features or prices. While financial services decisions are not made spontaneously, timing is extremely important.

As with most services, the most common selection factor is word-of-mouth referral. This is not surprising, since most people don't have an objective way of judging the quality of financial advice, insurance claims handling, or other types of services. When seeking the services of a stockbroker, pension adviser, private bank, or hedge fund manager, both institutional and consumer buyers seek the advice of their peers.

Cost Doesn't Matter Very Much

Because financial services decisions are often made without comparison shopping, the cost of a given service is often a less important consideration than convenience, reputation, or other factors. Most banks offer different tiers of pricing; consumers will generally decide on one tier or another, rather than comparing pricing within each tier at different institutions. Take, for example, a consumer looking for free checking. If a commercial bank branch is the closest and it offers free checking with a minimum of $2,500 in deposits, the consumer may choose to do business with that bank, at that tier of service, rather than walking an extra few blocks to a savings bank that offers free checking with no minimum. The convenience of the closest branch outweighs the cost of lost interest on the funds on deposit.

In some areas of financial services—notably, investments—consumers may focus on return and ignore costs, even though costs will affect return. In mutual funds, for example, management fees for the same type of fund can vary by more than a percentage point, as personal finance experts have been telling the public for years. But very few investors pay attention to management fees, 12b-1 fees, or even sales loads that can deduct 5 percent or more from the investment before the money is ever put to work. Even on the institutional side, returns trump fees. Top hedge funds may take as much as 50 percent off the top, but if returns are sufficiently high, investors are willing to share 50/50 the return on their own money.

The Advantage of Being the Low-Cost Provider

John Bogle, former chairman of Vanguard Funds, has been a voice in the wilderness calling for a reduction in management fees for mutual funds. He has pointed out, quite sensibly, that fee structures should have some connection to assets under management: A fund with few assets may need to charge higher fees to cover its costs and generate a profit. But even as assets double and triple in some funds, the percentages charged for management fees stay the same, thus doubling or tripling profits to the fund manager.

For the Vanguard Group, the failure of many consumers to pay attention to management fees has provided the money manager with a potent product differentiation as an extremely low-cost provider. There are seemingly enough consumers who *are* fee-conscious to have made Vanguard the No. 1 mutual fund investment company in the United States.

Vanguard Group's campaign in the late 2000's, created by Y&R Brands, was among the few to differentiate based on price.
Source: Investment News, 2010

"Stickiness" of Money Decisions

Online merchants refer to their sites as "sticky" if the visitors stick around for a while once they get there. Most financial services are "sticky" in the sense that once a purchase decision has been made, the buyer tends to stay with the product even when the reason for the initial decision is no longer valid. Thus, consumers who chose a bank that was nearby will continue to bank with the same company even after they have moved to another location that may be further from the nearest branch. Or an investor who chose a fund because it was a top performer will continue to hold the fund's shares even after it has become a performance also-ran.

For marketers, this customer loyalty (inertia is probably a more apt term) is a boon, since retention rates are generally higher than in other industries. One British study showed defection rates of 3 percent annually for banks, compared with a 15 to 20 percent defection rate for business in general. U.S. bank attrition rates are estimated at 10 to 12 percent, still below most other industries.[3]

The reasons for the "stickiness" of financial services are not primarily marketing-driven, however. The reality is that for many consumers, it is simply too much trouble to change service providers. It's easy to switch toothpaste brands or to go to a different grocery store. It's much more of a hassle to move your money from one bank or broker to another. Or consider refinancing a mortgage; the costs and paperwork make doing so such a time-consuming and expensive proposition that few people bother to refinance unless rates have dropped significantly. This inertia is particularly evident in the institutional market. A corporation doesn't lightly change benefits providers or lenders, for example, because there is an enormous cost in doing so.

For marketers, this inertia presents many opportunities. First, the costs of acquiring a new customer can be amortized over many years. Thus, more money can be devoted to acquisition versus retention marketing. Because the financial marketer doesn't need to spend great sums of money to keep customers from defecting, there are numerous opportunities to gain greater "share of wallet" among this captive audience. These opportunities include relationship building to increase cross-sales, as well as opportunities for referrals.

Are financial marketers making the most of their advantages? Airlines have spent billions of dollars to build customer loyalty, something that financial services companies take for granted. Not only do many financial services marketers have a near captive audience in their current customers, but they also have the opportunity to communicate with these customers on a regular basis—in the branches, through monthly statements, online, and through service calls. And consumers are likely to open a piece of mail or respond to a phone call from their financial institution.

What's more, financial services companies have an enormous marketing advantage in that they generally know a great deal about their customers. In fact, the credit card industry was among the first to segment its markets based on profitability analyses, because it readily had the data in hand to determine not only who was using the product, but also how often, how quickly they were paying off, and what they were spending their money on. Banks and brokerage firms have more information about their customers than most other types of marketers—information like value of their home, age, income, borrowing behavior, and much more. A savvy consumer marketer like Coca-Cola could turn such information to huge advantage.

As pointed out by Booz & Company in a report on Financial Services Return on Investment (ROI), "the paradox of FS marketing is that the industry has access to more marketing data than nearly any other industry, but it is much more difficult

Learning Marketing Lessons from Schwab

Unlike many financial companies, Charles Schwab & Co. is a leader in marketing practice, both in product innovation and in marketing techniques. Schwab was among the first firms to systematically use online methods to attract, retain, and cross-sell customers. Its sophisticated use of the Internet has been far ahead of most of its competitors. For example, many financial companies talk about "one-to-one" marketing online but send e-mail communications that are not customized. Schwab, on the other hand, offers individualized monthly comparative performance reports for each fund held by the shareholder.

Prepared by the Schwab Center for Financial Research

Data as of 09/30/2011 Symbol - Fund Name (Inception Date)	Actual Return 1 Mo	1 Yr	Average Annual Total Return 3 Yr	5 Yr	10 Yr	Since Inception
Morningstar Category: **Foreign Large Blend**						
Category Average	-13.16	-12.78	-2.14	-3.83	4.33	N/A
MSCI EAFE NR USD	-9.53	-9.36	-1.13	-3.46	5.03	8.84
<u>SWISX</u> - Schwab International Index (05/20/1997)	-10.96	-10.31	-2.86	-3.53	4.53	2.56
Morningstar Category: **World Bond**						
Category Average	-4.28	0.30	7.80	6.15	6.55	N/A
BarCap US Govt/Credit TR USD	1.03	5.14	8.41	6.52	5.74	8.03
<u>LSGLX</u> - Loomis Sayles Global Bond Retail (12/31/1996)	-5.01	0.94	9.36	6.25	8.23	6.76
Morningstar Category: **Large Growth**						

to capture, analyze, and act on this data." The reasons for this paradox, Booz suggests, is that "Consumer Products companies do not contend with complexities such as interest-rate climates, variations in customer profitability, or dependence upon sales force incentives to drive product mix."[4]

While the Booz report indicates that financial companies have steadily increased their marketing budgets as a percentage of sales, marketing is often viewed as a cost center rather than a strategic investment. Financial services companies have traditionally been among the least marketing-focused industries. Segmentation and target marketing in these industries is often at an unsophisticated level. Retirement providers, for example, often fail to segment their participants by retirement life cycle stage (starting out, mid-career, pre-retirement, etc.), even though this information is easily accessible and useful to both provider and participant. Very few financial marketers (with the exception of credit card companies) attempt to "slice and dice" the kind of narrow demographic segments that consumer products marketers routinely pursue. Using the information a company has about its customers to develop products, services, and communications to meet those customers' needs isn't done often or well enough.

Because there are "silos" between credit and debit products or between competing sales forces, information is often not shared across an institution.

Similarly, financial institutions sometimes fail to exploit their ability to communicate regularly with customers. Although there are exceptions, few financial institutions have created compelling reasons for their customers to read their messages. The airlines, for example, have developed very successful online programs that provide alerts to bargain airfares. The weekly e-mail from airline to customer creates an opportunity for brand building and developing customer loyalty. Some online brokerage firms provide a similar service with investment alerts, and there have been other creative uses of the Internet and mobile messaging, but the vast majority of financial institutions passively wait for their customers to contact them.

Legal and Regulatory Constraints

As if financial marketers didn't have it tough enough dealing with the structural issues of the industry, they must also answer to a higher authority. Financial services are among the most regulated of industries, at the federal, state, and industry-watchdog level. These regulatory constraints affect numerous marketing decisions. For example, the Financial Industry Regulatory Authority (FINRA) must review all marketing materials created by investment companies. Not only does this oversight govern which claims may be made in those materials but it also affects decisions about timing of materials (to allow for review) and even layout and design ("small print" is regulated as to size).

As another example of how regulatory constraints limit marketing decisions, consider that insurance products have to be approved on a state-by-state basis. If a product is not available in a particular state, this will complicate advertising strategy, since national advertising may not be cost-effective. Or the timing of bringing a new mutual fund to market will be dictated by Securities and Exchange Commission (SEC) regulations, which mandate approval by the fund company's own shareholders before the product can be distributed.

Successful Financial Marketing

You don't have to be a genius to market financial services, but it couldn't hurt. Some institutional investment firms employ quantitative analysts who are referred to in the industry as "rocket scientists." These prodigies come up with complex formulas to predict or hedge market behavior. But once they create their Einsteinian product, someone has to market it. Understanding and communicating the work of geniuses is just one of the many challenges facing the financial marketer.

Whether it's applying the latest marketing tools or mastering clinical psychology, the task of the financial marketer is unlike that of any other professional. Unfortunately, there is no Nobel Prize for marketing, but there are quantifiable rewards for marketing success. The following chapters will help you better plan your marketing and sales strategy to achieve that success.

Fitting "Small Print" into a Broadcast Spot

The regulations that govern the financial services industry often have a direct impact on marketing programs and their execution. In this highly regulated industry, making space for required disclosure information can become a nightmare unless you plan ahead. You have to arrange for compliance and legal review of all material, and adequate time for these reviews must be factored into production schedules and launch dates. Furthermore, you must design disclosure language into your layout as well as allow for it in your broadcast advertising. Failing to do so will not only cost you time but also potentially thousands of dollars in new creative and production costs.

The disclosure information for one large financial services company was so extensive that it required 15 seconds of a 30-second radio commercial. The choice was to either reduce the amount of disclosure or buy more airtime. After much discussion, agreement was reached on a way to tighten the disclosure language—to 10 seconds, leaving 20 seconds of the 30-second spot for the sales message.

Getting the Most from This Book

This book is meant for three types of readers: (1) marketers and managers at financial services companies, (2) those who sell financial products or services, and (3) students and those who are looking for positions in financial services marketing and sales. The chapters that follow are organized into two sections. Section 1 addresses the strategic tools of financial marketing, including segmentation, targeting, positioning, branding, competitive analyses, strengths-weaknesses-opportunities-threats (SWOT) analyses, market research, and market planning. Section 2 covers specific financial marketing tactics, including online and offline advertising, public relations, sponsorships, direct marketing, personal selling, trade shows, and customer-retention tactics.

The appendix, "Applying Marketing Principles to Sales Practice," is a bonus feature designed to help sales professionals visualize how the lessons outlined in the chapters can be applied in real-life situations.

Readers who are already marketing practitioners may be familiar with the strategic principles outlined in section 1. Although a review of these principles and the associated case studies will be valuable, such readers may wish to skip ahead to the tactical chapters. For those in sales or in training, strategy is often overlooked. Many product managers or sales executives, eager to fill their pipelines with prospects, jump over the planning process and start implementing tactics. "I need more prospects, so I'll advertise," the thinking often goes. But advertise where? With what offer? In expectation of what?

Implementing marketing tactics without a strategic plan is like building a home without a blueprint. It may work—or the edifice may collapse in the first strong wind. Consider the sales manager who spent tens of thousands of dollars to get prime space at a trade show only to find that the attendees were not his customers but his competitors.

Strategic marketing serves to prevent these kinds of mistakes. By identifying target segments, the marketer avoids wasting money on prospects who will never buy or on buyers who will never be profitable. Market research can help determine the characteristics of potentially profitable segments in order to reach them more effectively. Competitive analyses, environmental analyses, positioning, and branding strategies can help determine how a company or product is viewed in the marketplace and what opportunities exist to build greater market share. In other words, planning before making any promotional decisions helps maximize the return on investment of every marketing dollar. Strategic marketing asks the questions who, what, when, where, and why. Only after answering these questions, can you successfully implement the tactical hows that are addressed in section 2.

For resources on financial marketing, including articles, case studies, and links to relevant sites, see our related Financial Services Marketing Handbook blog at www .fsmhandbook.com.

Notes

1. Pertrac 2008 (www.pertrac.com)
2. Michael Pompian. *Behavioral Finance and Wealth Management.* Hoboken: John Wiley & Sons, 2006.
3. Tina Harrison, *Financial Services Marketing* (Edinburgh: Pearson, 2000). Harrison's source for the 15 to 20 percent attrition rate is a Bain and Company study, published by F.F. Reichheld and W.E. Sasser, "Zero Defections: Quality Comes to Services," *Harvard Business Review*, September/October 1990, 105–111. For the 3 percent British bank attrition rate, she cites *Financial Times*, November 16, 1998. American data on bank attrition are from Patrick Dalton, Customer Retention, *ABA Bankers News*, July 5, 2005.
4. "Understanding Marketing ROI in Financial Services," Booz & Company report, 2007. Used with permission. www.booz.com/global/home/what_we_think/reports_and_ white_ papers/ic-display/41901746

Strategic Market Planning

CHAPTER 1

Segmentation

Segmentation is the most basic marketing strategy. Although all marketers segment to some degree (even if they aren't aware they are doing so), many financial companies, particularly on the institutional side, do not take full advantage of segmentation strategies to improve their marketing effectiveness. Most institutional sales executives work through personal industry contacts and industry gatherings, thus segmenting on a de facto basis by industry. For example, a bond salesperson will tend to know and interact with others in the bond industry. In fact, some institutional markets are so limited—to take a random example, defined-benefit pension plans with more than $250 million in assets—that salespeople can list every potential client company by name.

Even within such narrow market segments, there is usually a benefit to segmenting further. A salesperson only has so much time and needs to prioritize. Circumstances change; threats and opportunities arise. Segmenting means answering questions such as these:

- Which organizations do business with your company?
- Can your clients be further divided into those that are in solid relationships and those that need to be cultivated?
- Can clients be analyzed by the types of products they currently buy and others that they may need?
- Can they be segmented by current or potential future profitability, allowing the sales force to spend more time with the 20 percent of clients that provide 80 percent of profitability?
- Which organizations do business with your competitors? Can these companies be further divided into those who are unlikely to change suppliers in the near future and those that may be looking for a change?

So Many Prospects, So Little Time

A group within a large institutional brokerage invented a new type of institutional cash fund, similar to a money market fund, but offering some unique advantages. While it was successful among the sales force serving the middle market, the capital-markets sales force ignored it. The inventors decided to set up their own business to market the product. As there were only three principals, their time was limited. A marketing plan devised by an outside consultant recommended the following segmentation strategies:

- Limit potential clients geographically, so that the principals would not have to travel extensively (geographic segmentation).
- Concentrate on the middle market, because it had already shown its viability and because it could be reached through marketing tactics other than direct sales, such as online advertising, public relations, direct mail, and other means (demographic segmentation by size of business).
- Select larger institutions in a few key industries (such as local governments) to target for sales calls. The industries were selected based on ease of reach, potential profitability, and other factors (demographic segmentation by industry).

However, the group did not act on this advice and continued to sell on an ad hoc basis through personal contacts, referrals, and serendipity. As a result, the three were constantly chasing perceived opportunities, wasting a good deal of their time. Unfortunately, serendipity was not enough, and the business never met their expectations.

The End of Undifferentiated Markets

On the consumer side, it is better understood that the market is no longer undifferentiated. Back in the 1950s, there was a mass market. There was one kind of Coke, and Coke sold it to everyone in the world in the same way. But those were also the days when television consisted of three networks and most people read mass-market magazines like *Life*.

Today, the *mass market* is made up of multiple niche segments that do not intersect. Girls ages 12 to 15 read different magazines, watch different television programs, go to different web sites, and join different Facebook groups than do older or younger girls. Television has splintered into hundreds of cable channels, devoted to specific demographic market segments (women, Hispanics) or niche interests (golf, Wall Street, cooking, fashion). Very few magazines reach a heterogeneous audience—today magazines are targeted to ever-narrower niches (black entrepreneurs, retirees in Florida).

Very few companies can afford to be everything to everyone any more. Even companies with mass-market products (like basic checking accounts) segment their

Targeting for Referrals

A financial adviser of Indian origin sold an investment plan to a relative, who was an Indian physician. The adviser began getting business from colleagues of this relative, who were also Indian physicians. Because the segment was potentially highly profitable and there was little competition seeking its business, the adviser decided to target this group more systematically. He offered seminars on financial planning for physicians at local hospitals that had a high percentage of Indian doctors. He sought an invitation to speak at a national conference of Indian physicians. He offered to write a regular column on financial planning for physicians in a magazine targeted to Indians in the United States. The success of these efforts was not surprising, since most people seek referrals from those they trust. Because this market segment was small and easily reached, the adviser soon did not need to actively market at all, as referrals from current clients enabled his business to prosper.

markets so that they can focus their limited marketing dollars on the most profitable segments. Mass advertising today is often costly and its effectiveness needs to be carefully considered. One example where the cost benefit is often debated is purchasing airtime for the Super Bowl. For this mega event a 30-second spot recently cost $3 million for airtime, plus the advertiser likely spent an additional million dollars in production costs. While E*TRADE has generated much buzz from its Super Bowl "baby" advertising, only a small fraction of the reported 110 million viewers fall into the company's target market. Most of the ad costs are probably not recouped directly by Super Bowl viewers signing up for accounts.

Choosing Target Segments

Targeting is picking the actual market segments you want to go after. The benefits of targeting include the following:

- Targeting helps you identify the media that best reach your target segments. When you've identified a particular segment (for example, young professionals just starting out in practice), you can more easily determine the media that best reach these markets (for example, law or medical school alumni magazines and web sites).
- Targeting helps build referral business. People tend to affiliate with people who are similar in interests or demographics. They are also likely to refer businesses to their friends and follow each other's purchasing patterns, whether through word of mouth, Tweeting, or other social networking.

One Hundred Thousand Market Segments at Capital One

How many segments are enough? As many as you need. One good reason to create ever-smaller cells is to test results of different variables on offers. Capital One, for example, went from being a small, relatively unknown institution into one of the world's largest—and most profitable—credit-card issuers in a few short years. The company is a pioneer in customer segmentation, using profitability analysis to determine which segments to target.

The company developed proprietary analytical tools to tailor its products to the appropriate customers and ensure that each customer is serviced efficiently—and profitably. Capital One used these models to determine which combination of product, price, and credit limit could be profitably offered to customers who could be segmented by a wide range of publicly available credit and demographic information.[1] Capital One ran more than 45,000 tests annually. From these test results, Capital One divided its market into one hundred thousand different segment or product combinations. Do the small differences in scores merit this much data handling? It has certainly paid off for Capital One. In 2011, Capital One was the fifth largest credit-card company in the world, in terms of credit issued, after Bank of America/MBNA, Chase, Citi, and American Express, with a 6.95 percent share of the U.S. market.

Source: What a Capital Idea, *Banking Technology*, July–August 2002, 44; and http://seekingalpha.com/article/200673-world-s-top-10-credit-card-issuers from *CreditCards.com and Neilson Report, via CNBC.*

- Targeting specific market segments increases the potential return of your marketing dollars. It might seem obvious that when you buy a mailing list, you should limit it to people who have the ability to buy your product. Yet, at least one bank, failing to cross-analyze its own customer list, sent a solicitation for renters' insurance to homeowners who had mortgages with the bank! Targeting should help avoid such waste and irritation to customers.
- Targeting helps you narrow the focus of your message, making it more likely that the prospect will respond. Although the average direct mail offer today gets less than a 2 percent response[2], when the list, the offer, and the message are narrowly targeted, response can go up to 10 percent or more.
- Targeting enables organizations to build products designed for target segments and to avoid market segments where no appropriate products exist. An investment company that specializes in fixed-income funds is not going to have much to offer day traders looking for fast profits and shouldn't waste its money seeking them. However, if a target segment, such as retirees, is looking for a related product, like annuities, it may be sensible to investigate offering such products.

FIGURE 1.1 Segmentation Stages

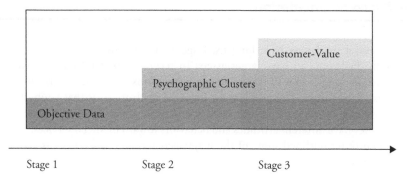

Methods of Segmentation

There are many ways to segment a market. The most common method is demographic, because demographic information is easy to acquire. Product purchase behavior (what a customer has purchased in the past) is another objective type of segmentation based on information that also is readily available. Other types of segmentation require more sophisticated data collection and analysis. Marketers usually begin with objective segmentation methods and develop these more sophisticated methods over time, as shown in Figure 1.1.

Objective Methods of Segmentation

Demographic Segmentation

Financial institutions targeting specific age groups are practicing demographic segmentation—the most basic kind of segmentation. Other examples of demographic segmentation include an effort by Wells Fargo to make its online services more accessible to the blind and visually impaired, a home mortgage–like product developed by HSBC that addressed religious law forbidding Muslims to pay or receive interest, and a sponsorship by several mutual funds (Calvert, Domini, TIAA-CREF) of a gay and lesbian conference.

The great advantage of demography as a segmentation variable is that it is based on observable, measurable characteristics. Demographic variables in the consumer market can include age, sex, race, religion, personal income, household income (HHI), marital status, number and ages of children, home ownership, education, professional status (type of job), language, ethnic group, physical disability, and sexual preference. In the business market, demography can include size of business (by number of employees, revenues, or other measures), type of industry, length of time in business,

Age-Based Segmentation

Many financial marketers have long used age as a segmentation strategy because older individuals tend to have larger assets. In recent years, banks and brokerages have started looking at how to reach younger generations, since they are the financial customers of the future. The problem for financial institutions is that young people do not transact or respond to the same marketing tactics as their elders. More critically, they have different attitudes and behaviors toward financial services. A 2006 study by Forrester outlined some of the major generational differences as shown in Table 1.1. below.

TABLE 1.1 Generational Differences in Attitudes toward Selecting a Financial Institution

More likely to:	Gen Y	Seniors
Consider price more important than brand name	•	
Prefer dealing with people		•
Rely on recommendations	•	

Source: Adapted from http://www.forrester.com/Research/Document/0,7211,39382,00.html

Seniors show the least interest in shopping around before making a purchase. They are the least likely to say that price is more important than brand name and are more comfortable dealing with people (instead of technology) when they shop or bank. Gen Y consumers are most likely to rely on recommendations when making a purchase. They also believe that price is more important than brand names.

ownership characteristics (public corporation, privately held), management structure (hierarchical or flat), and so forth.

Geographic Segmentation

Geography is also a basic, measurable segmentation variable. Clearly, a company that does business only in certain geographic regions (such as a local bank) would limit its target market to potential customers in that region. Geographic segmentation also applies to creation of sales territories and efforts to expand nationally or internationally, as well as to pinpointing potential markets by type of neighborhood, urban versus rural locales, single or multiple locations for businesses, and the like.

Geographic Segmentation for Flood Insurance

Demographic and geographic segmentation are useful because these characteristics are easy to act on. One particularly clever use of geographic data was an online promotion for State Farm insurance. It was targeted at visitors to Weather.com who live in regions of the United States that are usually warm but occasionally suffer cold spells. When weather forecasts for these regions predicted snow or freezing temperatures, a Flash ad from State Farm crossed their screen, with a warning about frozen pipes. A Flash image of a boy in a scuba suit and his dog, underwater, was the punch line.

State Farm targeted local weather.com visitors when freezing weather was forecast

Life-Cycle Segmentation

Another common method of segmenting a market is based on the fact that customers' needs change as they enter different phases of the life cycle: For example, young married couples are likely to buy a home, growing businesses are likely to need a line of credit. Although identifying potential clients by life-cycle phase is strongly correlated with marketing success, the data points are often difficult to find. If you're looking for people who have just bought a home (say, to target for a home equity product or mortgage insurance), it's easy to find this information. If you're looking for people who are thinking about buying a home, the task is much more difficult.

Life-Cycle Event—The First Job

Welcoming consumers into the labor force (and getting a shot at their first independent income) is a goal of many marketers. Visa and MasterCard offered pre-paid cards (also known as "stored value" cards) for fast-food restaurants and others to pay their young employees. Since teenagers seldom have checking accounts, paychecks are inconvenient. Prepaid credit cards can be used like any other credit card. For the bank that issues the card, acquiring consumers at the beginning of their working life increases the likelihood that they will remain customers for other products later.

Product Segmentation

When General Motors' Alfred Sloan called in 1924 for "a car for every purse and purpose," he was segmenting his customers to match his cars—Chevrolets for the young and less affluent, Cadillacs for an older, wealthier crowd, other brands in between. Banks have also traditionally segmented their markets by product—credit card customers are in one silo, home equity loan customers in another, and certificate of deposit owners in a third. From this rudimentary information, customer relationship management (CRM) systems are built, yielding valuable data on account size, profitability by product, purchasing patterns, usage (debit versus credit), number of products, churn and retention rates by product, transaction method (phone, online, in branch), and other variables.

Segmentation by Psychographic Clusters

Demographic, geographic, and purchase variables are relatively easy to find and use, but they have limitations. Take, as an example, two 30-year-old men with similar incomes and education. Both are married and childless, but one has $100,000 in investable assets, and the other has no savings. What variable explains this difference in behavior?

Attitudes and behaviors are much more difficult to observe and measure than demographics, but they can offer more insight into what customers actually buy and why. And by analyzing why customers have bought in the past, it is possible to project who would be most likely to buy in the future.

Knowing why customers buy is very helpful for creating targeted campaigns. For example, SouthTrust Bank's home equity line of credit direct mail solicitation was segmented by the purpose of the loan: Home improvement, debt consolidation, and children's education were the three leading categories. Knowing this made it easier to customize the messages for a direct mail campaign targeted to prospects in each of these segments.

Lifestyle Segmentation

Lifestyle segmentation operates on the principle that "birds of a feather flock together." Similarities of interests, attitudes, and activities are common among people who live in the same neighborhood—for example, suburban soccer moms often read the same magazines, shop in the same stores, and share political and social viewpoints with their neighbors. The tools that are used to group customers and prospects into attitude and behavioral segments include cross-tabulation analysis, data mining, predictive modeling, cluster analysis, and other statistical techniques. The resulting variables have many names, including psychographics, behavioral models, values-based analysis, and lifestyle analysis.

One common way of determining the lifestyle characteristics of one's customers is to overlay one's own database with a commercial "cluster analysis." Cluster systems, such as Neilsen Claritas' PRIZM and P$YCLE, Experian's MOSAIC, and ACORN in

---

Applying Cluster Analysis

Nielsen Claritas created a finance-specific lifestyle model. Called P$YCLE, it differentiates 58 clusters by financial behavior and characteristics. A cluster is a zip code–based group with similar demographic and behavioral characteristics.

Consider two clusters, both aged 25 to 44. "Fiscal Rookies" are mostly childless college graduates with median household incomes of $60,000. They have moderate levels of savings. While they own homes, these primarily white households carry debt from student and auto loans and first mortgages. They spend much of their income on active lifestyles, including skiing and racquetball. They tend to listen to rock music, read about fitness, and watch comedy shows.

Compare this group to "City Strivers," who are urban, young renters. Their median household income is $42,000 and they have very little saved. Diverse in both ethnicity and family type, most attended college and now work at a mix of white-collar and service jobs. They are paying off student, car, and personal loans. A majority have children, so most of their income goes to childrearing expenses. For leisure, they go to movies, roller skating, or dancing and buy family-friendly toys. Their interests are gaming and parenting, listening to rock, and watching reality TV shows.

Knowing which clusters your customers belong to, and which you would like more of, can determine what products are offered (home equity lines versus college savings accounts), which marketing channels to select (sponsorships of ski races versus baby shows), media placement (fitness web sites versus family web sites), and so forth.

Financial marketers can plug their own customers into these databases to help determine the characteristics of their target segments. Once these customers have been clustered, their common characteristics can be used to determine media, product, and message preferences.

Source: P$YCLE Segmentation Sample Report, Neilsen Claritas, 2010. www.claritas.com.

the United Kingdom, use census and other quantitative and qualitative data to divide countries into clusters, based on demographic and lifestyle similarities.

Business customers can also be segmented by psychographic criteria and buying behavior. For example, businesses can have different types of personalities: entrepreneurial, buttoned down, consensus driven. Decision-making styles can vary—in some businesses, decisions are made by one individual while in others they are made by committee. Purchasing decisions may be based on different personality factors: Some businesses seek name brands or added-value services, whereas others look for the cheapest solution. Some businesses are "innovators" or "early adopters," that like to be on the cutting edge. Others are followers or "laggards" in their adoption of new technology. The sales force needs information about important behavioral factors such as length of sales cycle, relationship (preferred provider versus competitive bidder), and expectations for delivery, maintenance, training, and other services.

Customer-Value Segmentation

When psychographic characteristics are combined with profitability data, organizations can develop deep knowledge of their customers. As customer relationship management systems have become capable of predicting and projecting, segmentation schemes have developed that can increase lifetime customer value—that is, both the length of a customer's tenure and the long-term profitability of that customer. For more on retention and customer value, see Chapter 11.

As an example, a bank took all the various data points it had collected about its customer base and then appended behavioral and attitudinal data. This combination of data enabled the bank to view customers and prospects in terms of potential profitability.

Table 1.2 shows two of the identified groups: the Asset Managers, who may not be currently profitable but have the potential to become so if more assets can be captured, and the Secure Traditionalists, who are the cash cows of the bank.

The insights provided by these segmentation methods are useful in several ways: They can help a company target new prospects who resemble their current best

TABLE 1.2 Lifestyle and Profitability Segments

	Attitudes	Behaviors	Characteristics
Asset managers	• Astute financial manager • Tax concerns • Interest rate sensitive	• Frequent transactor • Uses electronic banking • Uses many banks and non-banks	• High income/assets • Younger than average customer • Young children
Secure traditionalists	• Most loyal • Seeks value, convenience recognition, and personal service • Low price sensitivity	• Average transactor • Moderate electronic usage • Saving for a purpose	• Moderate income/high assets • Slightly older than average customer • College-age children • Owns valuable home

Subsegmenting the Ultra Wealthy

Wealth managers, private banks, hedge funds, and others who serve the Ultra-High-Net-Worth (UHNW) market tend to clump all prospects into one group: investable assets above $x. ($x can range from $1 million to $25 million or more.) A very small number of households fall into this segment—about 840,000 American households had $5 million or more in investable assets in 2008, according to Spectrem Group. So why bother further segmenting them? Surely, anyone with $5 million or more to invest is worth going after?

Yes, but how do you reach them? What are their goals and behaviors? What are their attitudes toward money management? What messages resonate?

Studies that analyze sub-segments of the UHNW market offer guidance. For example, one analysis divides the market by source and duration of wealth, as shown in Table 1.3.

TABLE 1.3 Stages of Wealth Evolution

Wealth maturation stage	Emergent (recent wealth)	Maturing (5 to 15 years' wealth)	Senior (inherited wealth)
Need for advice	High	Already have circle of advisors	Already have circle of advisors
Investment Products	Asset diversification	• Alternative investments • Intergenerational wealth transfer	• Endowments and foundations • Charitable bequests

Source: The Harrison Group, The Worth-Harrison Taylor Study of The Status of Wealth in America, © 2005. Cited in Andrea Trachtenberg and Evelyn Ehrlich, "America's new ultra-wealthy are not your father's multimillionaires." *Wealth Manager,* June, 2006.

customers. They can help cross-sell and up-sell current customers who are thought to have additional assets outside the institution. They can help retain current customers by predicting life-cycle or service issues that require intervention.

Behavioral segmentation can also help determine levels of service for current customers in order to maximize profitability. This must be done carefully, however. There have been a few public relations disasters when companies have too publicly announced that they were shifting unprofitable customers to cheaper methods of service, like ATMs or online access. Further, by making this information available to branch staff, there is the risk of inadvertently revealing potentially embarrassing information to customers. At the same time, if better service is to be offered to better customers, the customer-facing staff must be aware of which profitability "bucket" the customer falls into.

Finding Your Target Segments

The science of marketing comprises fact-based research, sophisticated statistical methods, testing of hypotheses, and analyzing results. The art of marketing is based on experience, imagination, and creativity. Both art and science must go into choosing target segments.

Any financial firm that has been in business for any length of time has three potential markets: current customers, prospective customers, and former customers. This last group is often overlooked, yet can be a significant source of new business for certain products. For example, a customer who has purchased an equity loan product in the past is an excellent prospect for a future equity line.

For start-up firms or companies that are expanding their markets, the task is more difficult. Rather than analyzing current customer patterns, they need to develop profiles of potential segments based on the variables most appropriate to their situation. For each profiled segment, research must determine the following:

- Market potential: What is the total size of the segment in dollars or units?
- Sales potential: What market share percentage of this segment can you reasonably expect to develop (over one or more years)?
- Competition: Who are the market leaders? What strengths and vulnerabilities make this an attractive segment?
- Ease of reach: How will you reach this segment? Are there identifiable media that match key variables?
- Cost: How much will it cost to reach this market? Can you afford it?
- Other resources: Do you have products that appeal to this market segment? Sufficient marketing resources and expertise?
- Fit: Does this segment fit with your organization's objectives? Are there conflicts or synergies with other client segments? Are there changes in the environment that will make this segment more or less desirable in the future?

Segmentation Checklist

Use the checklist below to identify the important characteristics of your own markets—current and targeted for development.

- ❑ Demographic variables
- ❑ Financial variables (such as total investable assets, size of payroll)
- ❑ Geographic variables
- ❑ Life-cycle variables
- ❑ Product/service needs
- ❑ Attitudes toward product/service
- ❑ Buying behavior
- ❑ Behavioral variables
- ❑ Belong to (social/professional groups/networks)
- ❑ Media (specific reading/viewing/online habits)
- ❑ Responsive to (type of marketing approach)
- ❑ Market potential

Get Your Customers to Tell You How to Find More Customers

Learn as much as you can about why your customers buy from you, how to get them to buy more, how to encourage them to refer others to your firm, and how to find more people like them. Here are some sample questions you might want to ask your best customers:

Needs Being Met

- Why did you begin doing business with this firm?
- How did you hear about us?
- What was your initial impression?
- What is your impression now?
- What would you say are our greatest strengths compared with our competitors?

Needs Not Being Met

- What are you dissatisfied with?
- Are there products or services that our competitors offer that we don't?
- Would you buy these services if we offered them? (How many? How often?)

Generating Referrals

- Have you told colleagues and friends about our services? Why? Why not?
- Would you consider doing so in the future? Would you do so if you were given a discount on a future service?

Finding Similar Customers

- Follow up on how they came to you in the first place. Were they referred? By whom? Why?
- Who else might be interested in this type of service? Try to get referrals to specific decision influencers (like accountants or lawyers) or specific organizations (trade and professional associations, alumni groups, social organizations, neighborhood groups).
- If the customer came as a result of a marketing campaign, get specific details about the media that made them aware of your offering. Particularly in the institutional arena, find out what web sites or trade media your customers read for professional development, which trade shows or conferences they attend, whether they receive direct mail or unsolicited e-mail, as well as any personal information that might be appropriate (for example, if they are avid fishermen or active in a particular charitable organization).

Identifying Current Market Segments

Your best prospects will resemble your best customers. They usually buy for the same reasons and are reached through the same media and methods. Who are your most profitable customers? The old 80/20 rule still operates in most businesses: 80 percent of your revenues come from 20 percent of your customers.

What do your top 20 percent buy from you? How often? How long have they been customers? Look at last year's customer list. Are the same people still in your top 20 percent? If not, what happened? Why did some of them leave? Can you get them back if you address the issues that concern them? Are any of your other top customers likely to leave? Can you save them?

What characteristics do your top 20 percent have in common? Do they have similar demographics or other observable characteristics? Can you do a cluster analysis to find out where they live, what web sites they visit, or watch on TV? Are they in similar types of business? Do they belong to the same organizations? Do they have common relationships with lawyers, accountants, or other professionals?

How did they become customers in the first place? Was it through personal referrals, a mailing list, a web site, attendance at a trade show? This is critical information, and you should always enter this data when you first acquire a new customer. There are several ways to collect more detailed information about your customers:

- Surveys. Create a short questionnaire with key items of importance to your business (see box). If yours is a relationship business, you can call or e-mail your customers to ask if they are willing to participate. If you have a physical place of business, you can provide survey forms to waiting customers or have a staff member approach customers to fill out a survey.
- Informal Q&A sessions. You may want to talk informally to your top customers or arrange a breakfast meeting of five or six top customers for an informal focus group. Chances are they will be flattered to be asked. If you feel a need to provide an incentive, you can offer to make a donation to their favorite charity. You should also contact former customers to find out why they left.
- Industry gossip. Your sales force, suppliers, even your competitors can provide invaluable information about your markets. Go to sales conferences and trade shows. Even if you don't exhibit, you will pick up the latest inside information.
- Have a cluster-based overlay done on your customer database. If you have enough clients to make this worthwhile, you can get all kinds of interesting information about them, from what they do in their spare time to how much their homes are worth.

Notes

1. "The Customer Profitability Conundrum: When to Love 'Em or Leave 'Em," Knowledge at Wharton (2002), http://knowledge.wharton.upenn.edu/sandb/120402.html
2. Response rates for letter-sized envelopes, for instance, had a response rate in 2010 of 3.42 percent for a house list and 1.38 percent for a prospect list. DMA 2010 Response Rate Trend Report. http://www.the-dma.org/cgi/dispannouncements?article=1451

CHAPTER 2

Positioning and Branding

Segmentation and positioning are basic strategies of marketing and apply to every product and service. If you don't know who your prospects are, you can't go after them. If you don't know who you are, your customers won't either. Briefly put, positioning is determining how you want others to view your company, product, or service in relation to your competition. These others can be your target markets, your sales reps, your vendors, your community, your investors, your employees. Positioning—along with its close cousin, branding—defines who you are, what values you communicate, how you're different from others offering similar product sets, and why your constituencies should prefer you to your competitors.

Positioning Strategy and Differentiation

The easiest way to define who you are is by comparison and contrast with your competitors. What do they stand for? What do they offer their markets? Do you offer the same or different qualities? This exercise is called *differentiation*—determining how you are unlike your competitors.

Consider consumer banking as an example. Until fairly recently, there were two kinds of consumer banks: large banks with lots of branches but impersonal service, and small banks with personal service but few branches. Then some marketing genius came along and thought, "Why not combine personal service with lots of branches?" The result was a new wave of consumer-friendly banks like TD Bank, Umpqua Bank, and a growing number of regional banks that are increasingly focusing on service as a key differentiator. These businesses position themselves against their competitors to come up with a new and better bank.

Products that are undifferentiated are considered commodities, like grains or metal ores. A commodity market is one in which all products are the same (gold is gold) and cost the same. It doesn't matter to the marketplace how much it costs to extract the metal from a particular gold mine—you'll get the same price per ounce as your competitors.

Most companies want to avoid having their products turn into commodities. Even items that were once treated as commodities—basic checking, for example, are now being differentiated.

When Is a Toaster an Added-Value Differentiator?

With most bank deposit accounts offering similar terms and interest rates, some banks have gone back to a very old-fashioned means of differentiating their products—the account-opening gift. In the 1950s, you would get a radio, toaster, or some other small appliance when you opened a savings account. Today, with many more banks doing away with no-fee checking accounts, and all looking to bring in new high deposit customers, "gift giving" has become an art. Premiums for account opening have become more sophisticated than in the old days. Today's customer cannot just open an account and walk away with a gift. The idea is not just to capture a new client but also to keep them, so gifts come with qualifications such as a minimum amount of the initial deposit, the term the money must be kept for, or bundled services such as free checking with direct deposit.

Giftsforbanking.com rewards new CD customers, based on deposit amount and the term of the CD, with a choice of cookware, appliances, flat-screen TVs, cruises, and for the adventurous and romantic, a hot air balloon ride for two with champagne. Credit cards may offer free miles after the first purchase. Some companies team up with non-financial vendors, such as Apple, to cross-market.

According to one former Wells Fargo executive, banks have gone back to giving gifts for account openings because, with deposit accounts being virtual commodities, "How are you going to be remembered and move potential customers to come to you?" Gifts not only "build desire and move the purchase but build the brand image as well."

The most effective gift—and the one most often offered—is cold, hard cash. Many banks offer new accounts $100 or more based on a three-month average balance minimum. But sometimes gifts can be more memorable. Citigroup, for example, gave away gold and crystal pendants commemorating the Chinese New Year to customers at branches in Chinese neighborhoods who maintained balances of $15,000 or more. Bank of America geographically segmented its gifts, giving Boston customers tickets to Red Sox games and New York customers discounts on Broadway shows. PNC Bank was successful with a promotion that made a $25 donation to a local charity chosen by the customer. Said a PNC executive, "A lot of our competitors have undifferentiated products and need premiums to stand out. When we provide premiums, we want them to be tightly linked with our stance in the community."

Source: Jeremy Quittner, "Giveaways, an Old Bank Concept, Back in Vogue," *American Banker*, May 29, 2002, 10A.

There are many ways to differentiate. Some points of difference are tangible: price, selection, terms, and delivery time. Some are intangible: quality of service, expertise, image, value, and status. Some points of differentiation are inherent in your product or service. Mutual funds, for example, compete largely on the basis of investment return. If your fund is beating its peers, more investors will be interested in your products.

Companies can add value to their products in order to differentiate. Returning to the mutual fund example, the Vanguard Group has differentiated itself from its competitors by charging very low management fees, thus becoming a price leader (see the Introduction). Other companies differentiate by adding broader fund selections, like the fund supermarket approach pioneered by Charles Schwab.

Still others add value by offering online financial planning services or other unique online functions. For example, Fidelity and T. Rowe Price were leaders in offering retirement calculators that help investors determine how much to save. As with most differentiators, competitors try to keep up and the differential advantage may not last long.

Determining Positioning Strategy

If a company is offering a new product or service, it must determine early on how it will position itself with respect to both its target markets and competitors. Consider an investment manager who is setting up a new hedge fund. The process would consist of the following steps:

1. Examine strengths. (For example, experience in international hedging strategies.)
2. Determine target market need. (Is there a need in the marketplace that is not adequately being met? Would a fund of hedge funds be interested in adding an international specialist to its roster?)
3. Analyze the competition. (Who else is offering international hedging strategies? What are each group's strengths and weaknesses?)

This can be set up as a grid, as shown in Table 2.1. The rows show the characteristics that are important in the marketplace. The columns are for your company or product and its major competitors. The goal is to see where there is potential to differentiate.

In the example, New Hedge Fund is superior to its most direct competitors in its partners' experience in the international markets and in their previous jobs with well-known fund managers. Their most recent 12-month performance (at previous jobs) was about average for their peer group, but the partners have performed better

TABLE 2.1 Sample Positioning Strategy Grid

Target market needs	New Hedge fund	Competitor A	Competitor B
Expertise in foreign hedging	B	P	P
Value of principals' experience	B	P	W
Most recent 12-month performance	P	B	P
Performance consistency	B	P	W
Fees	Not yet determined	B	W
Marketing strength	W	B	P

P = Parity, B = Better than competition, W = Worse than competition

than average over time. The biggest negative is that New Hedge Fund has no money to support a sales force and is competing with relatively well-known firms. An open question is whether to charge more, less, or the same as its competitors.

An exercise of this type provides insight into how to distinguish one's own company from competitors, using attributes that matter to target markets.

Once you've established your positioning strategy, you need to make sure that all elements of your product and marketing adhere to it. A private bank is going to have a very different look and feel than a mass-market bank. Its client offices will be deeply carpeted, and the walls will be covered with fine art. Its marketing materials will be elegant and sophisticated rather than bright and fun. Client-facing staff will have advanced degrees and will dress and act like the professionals they are. Such formality would be out of place in TD Bank, which bills itself as "America's most convenient bank." The atmosphere is more casual: unbarred teller windows offer a friendly feel (despite making the bank a greater target for robbers). Free loose-coin counters for customers, dog biscuits for pet owners, and green plastic TD piggybanks for children encourage walk-ins. Positioning means knowing who you are and making sure that the face you present to the world is how you see yourself when you look in the mirror.

Developing a Positioning Statement

Many companies undertake a positioning exercise to ensure that they are presenting a consistent face to all their constituencies. One company in the alternative investment arena undertook a process led by their chief marketing officer (CMO). It began with in-depth interviews with all senior managers, selected client-facing sales executives, research analysts and others, that asked the following questions:

- How would you describe our company? If you were charged with selling the company, what are the highlights of the story you would tell?
- How would you describe the business the company is in?
- What are the benefits we provide to our clients?
- What are the most important factors accounting for our success?
- Who are our competitors?
- What is the firm's greatest differential advantage over the competition?
- What are our firm's strengths and weaknesses?
- How would you describe the personality of the firm in three adjectives?
- What is your view of the company's mission?

After these interviews, the analysis continued with a roundup of the main competitors' positioning. An initial positioning statement was drafted, refined, and then distributed to all relevant parties. Following further revisions, the statement was tested in focus groups among key client segments. In all, the process lasted more than three months, but the end result was a positioning strategy statement that reflected both the reality of the company's identity to its markets and the hopes the company had for its future development.

Creating a Distinctive Brand Identity

There are many words tossed around to describe different aspects of this important concept. "Brand," "image," "corporate image," "reputation," "brand value," "identity," and "brand recognition" are some of them. Although one can quibble over precise definitions, in essence, all of these words refer to the same concept.

Most marketers use the terms *positioning* and *branding* interchangeably. However, this discussion chooses to look at branding as a further refinement of positioning. Positioning defines a company or product in relation to its markets and competitors. Branding attempts to create a unique perception, an emotional or intellectual bond between product and end user. All companies and products are positioned (even if by default). Not all companies or products can be branded.

As an example, Visa and MasterCard have similar positioning in the minds of their target markets: They are both perceived as mass-market, all-purpose credit cards, particularly when compared with American Express, which has a more upscale image. Most people perceive very little difference between them in terms of product features, pricing, or other tangible qualities. If you ask people which credit card they carry, some would have to look in their wallet to see if it was a Visa or MasterCard.

Nevertheless, Visa and MasterCard have very different brand images. Advertising is not the only factor in creating a brand image, but a strong advertising campaign can certainly create a values-laden brand image. For consumers, the difference between Visa and MasterCard likely comes down to their tag lines: "More people go with Visa" versus the 17-year-old, iconic "Some things are priceless. For everything else there's MasterCard."

A strong brand image, like that of American Express, has monetary value; it is a quantifiable corporate asset. This is true for several reasons:

- Brand image translates into profits because a branded product can command a higher price than an equivalent generic product. Many banks offer free credit cards, but because American Express is a preferred brand name, it can command a premium.
- A brand image provides a shorthand way of letting constituents know what to expect from the company. A brand image has a personality, and a perceived level of quality is associated with particular brands. Sales staff, recruiters, or investor-relations managers will have a far easier time getting an audience if their target markets are already familiar with the brand image. When an American Express account manager calls up a new prospect, it will be easier to get an appointment than if that same salesperson were representing an unknown company.
- It is much cheaper to introduce a new product, or brand extension, if it is attached to a familiar brand name, such as the American Express plum card, successfully introduced in 2007.
- Most important of all, a brand name is unique. It is one characteristic of your product that cannot be copied by your competitors.

Can A "Giant Vampire Squid" Have a Positive Brand Image?

Brand image may differ by market segments. In recent years, Goldman Sachs has become the personification of the evil bank to the broad public. After the market crash of 2008, Goldman Sachs was at the center of public and regulatory outrage—one common epithet for the firm was "giant vampire squid"—and paid a fine to the Securities and Exchange Commission (SEC) for failing to disclose to clients material information about collateralized debt obligations. Yet, to its core constituency—institutional investors—Goldman remains the gold standard. Based on many years of experience, Goldman Sachs is viewed by most institutional investors as "the smartest guys in the room." The strength of Goldman's brand image—and its policy of not commenting on and settling disputes out of court—carried it through the crisis with its core client base. It was ranked first among the most admired megabanks by *Fortune* magazine in 2010. "The public at large may still see Goldman as the poster child for the greed that sparked the financial crisis, but its reputation in the business world is stronger than ever" noted *The Wall Street Journal* in March, 2011. Two years after the crash, Goldman remained one of the top dealmakers, ranking number one globally and domestically in 2010.

Source: World's Most Admired Companies, http://money.cnn.com/magazines/fortune/mostadmired/2010/snapshots/10777

Not every product or company can be successfully branded. Traditionally, branding has been used for tangible consumer goods—soaps, soft drinks, cars. Very few financial services companies have widely known brand names. This lack of brand recognition for most financial services companies in the United States is borne out by *Fortune* magazine's "World's Most Admired Companies 2011" list, which includes no financial services firms among the top 10. Only a handful are in the top 50 list, including

American Express (20), JP Morgan Chase (23), and Goldman Sachs (25). One reason may be that financial services companies do not engage emotionally, unlike such brands as Apple and Starbucks.

Why is American Express a more recognizable name than other financial services firms? For one thing, American Express has had the same name since it was founded in 1850 and a consistent branding approach for most of that time. For another, AmEx has been a consistent advertiser and has had one of the longest-standing relationships with its advertising agency—Ogilvy & Mather—since the 1950s. It is probably no coincidence that the agency is a strong proponent of what it calls "360-degree brand stewardship." This means that every piece of communication that passes among AmEx, its internal audience, and its clients contains the same tone and look, whether annual reports or product packaging, advertising or training manuals, websites or signage.

Very few brand strategies have had such consistency over such a long period. (Merrill Lynch, with its bull logo and "bullish on America" tag line going back to the early 1970s, is another rare example.) Part of the reason for the scarcity of recognizable financial brand names is simply that many notable brand names routinely disappear in mergers and acquisitions.

Whose Name?

When Bank of America acquired Merrill Lynch in 2009, it faced a decision about how to name the new, combined entity. Both brands were well-known, but Merrill's was far older and more upscale. Bank of America used research from customers and potential customers in at least 13 countries before deciding to keep the Merrill Lynch name (and bull logo) for its consumer brokerage business, while calling the company's corporate and investment bank Bank of America Merrill Lynch.

Similarly, when Chase Manhattan Bank acquired JP Morgan, it took the more prestigious name, JPMorgan Chase, for its institutional business.

In the past, acquiring companies often absorbed even well-known brand names, as when UBS acquired Paine Webber and AXA acquired the Equitable. But failing to establish sufficient awareness of the new brand, AXA Financial eventually was renamed AXA Equitable in the United States.

With lesser known brands, the acquirers' name is usually used, sometimes causing problems for outside parties. Naming rights to the Philadelphia sports arena were originally bought by one bank, which was then taken over multiple times. Thus the CoreStates Center became the First Union Center, then the Wachovia Center, and then the Wells Fargo Center, providing lots of business for sign makers.

Creating a Brand Image

For a new company or product, or one without a recognizable brand image, the starting point is the name. Naming can have an enormous impact on a business's success or failure. For example, SmartyPig.com has been successful, in part because its name memorably calls to mind a piggy bank.

In a crowded marketplace, a memorable name can stand out. In the competitive hedge fund area, most funds are named after their founder, but some managers have attempted to stand out from the crowd with names like Pirate Capital and Grizzly Bear Fund. A clever pair took the name "Dalton" from their old prep school—and got calls from alumni who were interested in investing.

After the name is settled, the next step in branding is the corporate identifier or logo. A logo should be distinctive and easily recognizable. A logo can use a distinctive typeface, or it may have a visual motif, like Chubb's circle or Citibank's "umbrella."

"Borrowing" a Brand Image

Because it is so difficult to make a financial company stand out from its competitors, some companies have had success by associating with a better-known brand name. For example, many credit card companies "co-brand"—with airlines, car companies, online retailers like Amazon, and so forth. Customers may not remember whether they're carrying a MasterCard or Visa, but they do remember they get points toward a new car with GM or book with Amazon every time they use it.

Co-branding helps promote both brands. First, the advertising dollars are multiplied for both brands, as in the Disney Rewards Visa. Second, co-branding enables synergies, such as free publicity for Visa at Walt Disney World or Disney's name appearing on Visa's cards. There is also a "rub-off" effect, by which Visa benefits from Disney's distinctive brand identity. In fact, Disney's identity was seen as so valuable that Visa paid an estimated $20 million in initial licensing fees.

The strategy of co-branding is not limited to the consumer marketer. Pentegra Retirement Services has targeted strategic alliances to help build the brand image.

Because its target markets are primarily banks, the company sought out and won the endorsement of the American Bankers Association—a backing that it trumpets on its web site as a kind of "Good Housekeeping Seal of Approval."

Not all co-branding efforts work. Co-branding may dilute the effectiveness of a brand image, since it spreads the credit for a positive experience across two brands where normally there's only one. And if the experience isn't positive—even if it's the other brand's fault—it may reflect negatively on you. Associating your company's name with a losing team or a spokesperson who becomes controversial can have negative consequences for your brand image, as Accenture found in building its branding campaign around Tiger Woods.

Other ways to borrow a brand image are to use well-known names in advertising and promotion. For example, MetLife licensed the Peanuts comic-strip characters to lend a "warm and fuzzy" feel to its product. Companies have tried, with varying degrees of success, to use celebrity endorsers.

Another way to create a brand image is to use real clients or executives. Charles Schwab & Co. built its advertising and its brand image around the figure of Charles Schwab. "Tombstone" ads, which announce completed deals, are examples of using real client names to bolster the image of the investment bank.

Goldman Sachs, Merrill Lynch, and Smith Barney use a tombstone ad to co-brand a stock issue for AT&T

Supporting a Brand Image

In maintaining a brand image, the most important quality is consistency. Both tangibles (such as brochures or premiums) and intangibles (such as service standards) should conform to the brand image. A contents page from a brand guidelines manual is shown in Figure 2.1.

There must be consistency of message across all channels of communication, including these areas:

- Management communications through public relations (talking to the press) and investor relations (talking to analysts)
- Internal communications with employees, vendors, and investors
- Company history and leadership
- Brick-and-mortar look and feel (offices, signage)
- Image projected by employees
- Online image
- Corporate identity system: use of name, logotype or symbol, color, and typography

FIGURE 2.1 Branding Guidelines Contents

Copy Guidelines
Brand Visual Identity
Brand Signature
Brand Signature–Placement
Brand Tagline
Colors–Palette
Typography–Font Family
Typography–Usage Examples
Graphics–Photography
Graphics–Charts
Grid–Print
Examples–Print
Examples–PowerPoint
Examples–Web site
Examples–Email
Examples–Tradeshow Graphics

Perhaps most important, maintaining the value of a brand image requires actively avoiding negative messages. It is not always possible to control negative messages, but there are ways to stack the odds in one's favor:

- Practice honest and proactive communications with all constituencies, including the press
- Create proactive customer-satisfaction programs
- Maintain company standards through employee recruitment and training
- Create a positive workplace environment
- Contribute through philanthropy and public service to build "reservoirs of goodwill" that will carry a good company through bad times.

Defending the Brand

Before social media, maintaining one's brand image was largely a matter of policing usage within an organization. Now brands must be protected against punk'rs, bashers, and other online threats.

One commonly understood threat is phishing—a criminal attempt to lure customers to fake financial sites that look like real ones. While phishing is a security issue, it is also a marketing concern: If your customers don't trust messages from your brand, your brand image can be endangered.

Disgruntled customers and employees may punk or bash you: That is, set up a web site or social media page that trash talks your brand. Do a search on "Ihate(brandname)," "(brandname) sucks," and similar key words to see examples of damage and abuse from angry bloggers, Facebook users, YouTube posters, Tweeters, and others. Sometimes fakers even pose as legitimate representatives of an organization, sending out Tweets or posts supposedly from the real company. They may register for an account on a photo-sharing or other social media site using someone else's brand name or break into a legitimate account and send out unauthorized information. Handling this type of brand abuse requires monitoring online usage of your brand name carefully. See Chapter 8 on Social Media Marketing for more detail.

Competitors can also affect your brand through such stunts as traffic diversion—by, for example, using your brand name to place their own ads. One example of traffic diversion involved Smartypig.com, a popular online savings site. A Romanian company called Trustypig ripped off not only Smartypig's name but also its look and feel, creating a virtually identical web site to confuse potential customers (see Figure 2.2).

Smartypig fought back using social media. The bank's fans organized a brand hijack—an orchestrated use of blogs, search-engine optimization (SEO), and social networks like Twitter and FriendFeed to "hijack" Trustypig's brand's placement in search-engine listings. The goal was to let searchers know that Trustypig was not Smartypig. And the Twitter mob got results: Within days, search results of "Trustypig" alerted users to the ripoff.

FIGURE 2.2   A "brandjack" by Smartypig's fans alerted Google searchers to a scam

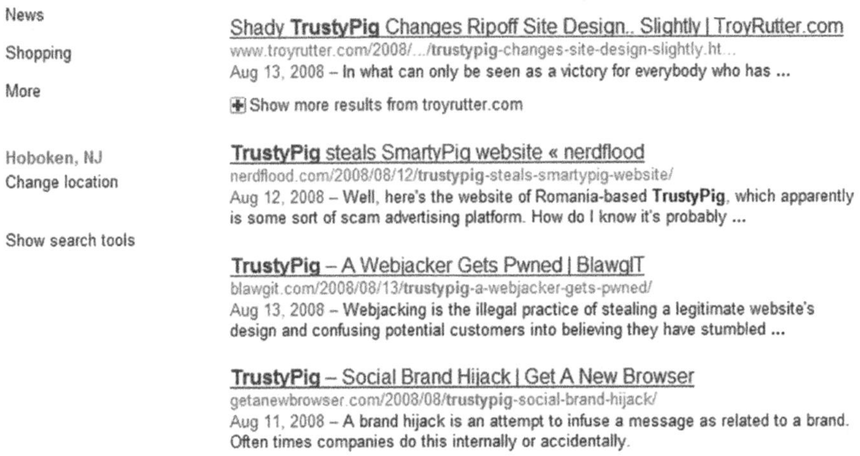

News

Shopping

More

Hoboken, NJ

Change location

Show search tools

Shady **TrustyPig** Changes Ripoff Site Design.. Slightly | TroyRutter.com
www.troyrutter.com/2008/.../**trustypig**-changes-site-design-slightly.ht…
Aug 13, 2008 – In what can only be seen as a victory for everybody who has …

⊞ Show more results from troyrutter.com

TrustyPig steals SmartyPig website « nerdflood
nerdflood.com/2008/08/12/**trustypig**-steals-smartypig-website/
Aug 12, 2008 – Well, here's the website of Romania-based **TrustyPig**, which apparently is some sort of scam advertising platform. How do I know it's probably …

TrustyPig – A Webjacker Gets Pwned | BlawgIT
blawgit.com/2008/08/13/**trustypig**-a-webjacker-gets-pwned/
Aug 13, 2008 – Webjacking is the illegal practice of stealing a legitimate website's design and confusing potential customers into believing they have stumbled …

TrustyPig – Social Brand Hijack | Get A New Browser
getanewbrowser.com/2008/08/**trustypig**-social-brand-hijack/
Aug 11, 2008 – A brand hijack is an attempt to infuse a message as related to a brand. Often times companies do this internally or accidentally.

CHAPTER 3

The Market Plan

The market plan is the center of the marketing process. Using the information on segmenting and positioning that you have already compiled, the market-planning process then asks you to set specific market objectives, as well as to develop a budget and ways to reach those goals. There are at least five important reasons to create a market plan. First, it saves time. Although marketers complain about the hours that go into the planning process, planning lets you align limited resources with your most important objectives. The second reason for a market plan is it lays out a clear direction for the entire marketing team. Rather than running in circles, the plan provides a road map that will help get the team from where it is today to where it wants to be at a given point in time.

The third reason is it allows management to weigh in and buy in to the programs and the corresponding budgets. It also offers an opportunity for every member of the marketing team, as well as critical partners, to fully understand the plan and the commitment expected to achieve success.

Fourth, it permits you to measure your results. Without a clear statement of your current situation and your objectives for the future, you can't determine whether or not you've succeeded. Even if elements of your plan fail, the information will be useful. The plan enables you to fix your mistakes and redirect the plan toward success. It's important to keep in mind that if a plan can't be measured, it can't be evaluated. If it can't be evaluated, success or failure is left to individual interpretation.

Finally, having a plan is more likely to lead to success. In large corporations, market planning is routine, but it is often considered too troublesome for smaller financial firms or for individuals, such as financial advisers, accountants, or consultants. Planning is associated with higher sales. In a survey of financial advisers in 2001, CEG Worldwide, found that the higher their income, the more likely they were to have a plan.

A market plan is a dynamic document that can change based on environmental factors as well as competitive product introductions, changes in competitor positioning, and shifts in your own company's strategic positioning. With each change, the market plan should be reviewed and adjusted. Even when things are proceeding as expected, the market plan should be reviewed regularly to determine whether schedules need to be updated, tactics revised, and responsibilities reassigned.

The type of marketing plan you develop will depend on the nature of your organization. A small business or individual practice will not have the resources to do as much market research as a large corporation. Its environmental and competitive analysis may be less developed. In a midsize company or a start-up, the marketing plan often will be developed along with the overall business plan. It will generally flow from the business plan and work in conjunction with other operating plans, such as finance, operations, and production.

In a large corporation, marketing plans may be developed by a marketing department, a line of business, a product group, a geographic region, or other business unit. Some institutions use a top-down approach to market planning, with a few key executives setting policy, which is then implemented in the field. In a bottom-up approach, each division, profit center, field office, or line of business may develop its own plan that is then "bought into" by senior management.

Researching Your Plan

Before you can write your plan, you need data. Market research data can be quantitative or qualitative. Quantitative research usually refers to surveys and other techniques that involve large sample sizes and resulting data that can be analyzed with some degree of statistical confidence. Qualitative research relies on small groups or individuals.

Quantitative Market Research

There are two primary types of quantitative data: That which you derive from your own customers and that gathered from public sources.

Customer information is invaluable in helping you answer questions like these:

- Who are your most profitable customers?
- What is your average customer-retention rate?
- How do buying patterns (amount, price, frequency) impact retention rates and profitability?
- Are there other factors that impact retention and profitability (such as demographics, psychographics, or life cycle)?

Public information commonly used in market research includes statistical data compiled by local and federal sources, business associations (like the Chamber of Commerce), and industry trade groups. For example, comparative banking statistics are available from sources such as the Federal Reserve Board and the American Bankers Association. Census data, industry information, and much more can be found by regular reading of business and trade publications, blogs, and various online sources. Competitors' web sites are also good resources for constructing comparative information on target markets, positioning, and marketing tactics.

Purchased research is available from market research firms. Syndicated research is often made available by subscription. For example, Dalbar and Cerulli Associates compile information of interest to retirement plan providers from regular surveys of third-party sales professionals, plan sponsors, and plan participants. Subscribers can receive information that is industry-wide or specific to their own company and its immediate competitors.

Customized research provides information based on the client's specific questions and is not shared with anyone but the client. A bank launching a new ad campaign, for example, might commission a survey to determine baseline awareness. After the campaign launches, the bank would conduct another survey to determine whether brand awareness and positive recognition have increased. The bank might also survey whether the ads were recalled (aided or unaided), and changes in purchase intent.

Qualitative Research

Sometimes marketers want answers to questions that can't be reduced to multiple choice. Determining client price sensitivity or how to effectively motivate third-party distributors usually involves qualitative techniques. Qualitative methods, such as focus

---

Using Research to Derive More Profit from Each Customer

If you could retain each customer an average of one month longer than you currently do, what would it add to your bottom line? A North Carolina mortgage lender discovered that keeping its customers on the books for one extra month increased its net annual interest income by 6 percent. Finding this metric through analysis of its own customer data was one use of market research. Putting it to work was the next step. The lender's data analysts began by determining which independent variables affected the duration of the loan. It discovered that profitability in lending (loan size multiplied by duration) had the highest correlation with the income of the borrower, the market value of the home, and the loan amount.

In addition to analyzing its own customer data, the North Carolina lender also looked at public information. From periodicals and trade association studies, it determined average retention rates for leading practitioners in order to determine whether its own retention rate was high or low. It was found to be about average. The bank engaged a consulting firm whose staff interviewed market leaders in noncompetitive industries (such as life insurance) to learn best practices for increasing retention.

One result was a "Scoring Guide for Payoff Prediction." This model enabled managers to estimate customer tenure and intervene before customers were lost. By communicating with profitable segments in appropriate ways and developing strategies to retain them, the lender used the data to improve bottom-line results.

Source: David Oshan and Kristin Triplett, "The Value of Retaining Customers," *Quirk's Marketing Research Review,* April 1994, www.quirks.com (article no. 062).

groups and personal interviews, are often used for evaluating branding strategies and marketing campaigns. Focus groups are usually done in a series, either over time or over geographical locations. One focus group may be atypical; it takes more than one to establish a pattern. For example, a brokerage company planned to launch a massive campaign targeted to high-net-worth women. Prospective materials, including promotional and educational tools, were shown to focus groups in New York, Chicago, Dallas, and Los Angeles. Each group consisted of eight women with net incomes above $100,000 and net assets above $500,000. While there were minor regional differences, there was substantial agreement among all the groups on key issues, which were then incorporated into the materials.

Recently, online focus groups have become increasingly popular. Similar to onsite focus groups, online versions include 8 to 12 participants and run approximately 60 to 90 minutes. Online sessions tend to be simpler to recruit and screen participants, due to pre-existing pools of willing participants. Online sessions are generally less expensive since travel and meals are not required. Keep in mind, online focus groups do not allow for the assessment of body language or probing for in-depth responses.

Observational research is another type of qualitative data gathering. For example, mystery shopping, in which a researcher poses as a customer, is a technique that can be used to evaluate the service proficiency of one's own employees or to learn more about competitors.

The Elements of the Plan

Although each organization will have its unique market plan format, there are elements that are common to most market plans. These include identifying your target segments, determining your positioning, setting objectives, developing tactics, establishing budgets and timetables, and setting up metrics for evaluating results.

SWOT Analysis

SWOT is an acronym for strengths, weaknesses, opportunities, and threats.

TABLE 3.1   Elements of the Market Plan

Executive summary: a synopsis of the plan and its key elements
Environmental analysis: SWOT (strengths, weaknesses, opportunities, and threats) analysis of your company and your competitors
Identification of your target segment(s) (see Chapter 1)
Analyzing your positioning in relation to your competition and establishing your branding strategy (see Chapter 2)
Establishing marketing objectives
Determining schedules, budget, human resources, responsibilities, and accountabilities
Setting implementation tactics
Identifying the metrics that will be used to track and measure success

---

Strengths are capabilities or resources of the organization (or product) that could be used to improve its competitive position. Weaknesses are the opposite. Strengths and weaknesses usually focus on the following items within the organization:

- Size of organization
- Reputation of organization
- Current market share of product
- Current market segments
- Ability to meet target market wants and needs
- Product or technological advantages/disadvantages
- Pricing advantage or disadvantage
- Market perception of product: positioning or brand image
- Operational strengths and weaknesses
- Budgetary constraints and types of resources available
- Management commitment
- Marketing/communications differentiation

SWOT Analysis for a Global Bank

A division of a multinational bank was charged with determining strategy for selling currency-transaction-processing services in Great Britain. This is a portion of its SWOT analysis:

TABLE 3.2 Sample SWOT Analysis

Strengths	Weaknesses
Demonstrated international expertise	Low market penetration
Offerings on par with the competition	Low market recognition
Internal client base to cover fixed expense	No decisive competitive advantage over other providers
Capability to provide multicurrency service	Sales force not familiar with product

Opportunities	Threats
Consolidation among British providers means fewer competitors	Declining global interest rates will reduce income but not operating expense
Potential outsourcing by smaller banks opens potential markets	Technology "fixed costs" continue to grow

From this analysis, the bank determined that its most likely potential target markets were smaller U.K. banks looking to outsource their transaction processing to a recognized multinational currency leader. The SWOT analysis also helped the bank identify areas of deficiency that needed to be addressed by the marketing team, such as sales training and brand-building efforts, in order to meet revenue objectives.

Opportunities and threats come from outside the organization. Opportunities are favorable conditions in the environment that can potentially produce rewards. Threats are external barriers that may prevent a company from reaching its objectives. Opportunities and threats may come from:

- Industry trends (industry growth, maturity, or decline)
- Economic factors (interest rates, business cycle, inflation)
- Political forces (wars, changes in leadership, new legislation, or court decisions)
- Regulatory forces (new or changing regulations)
- Technology
- Demographic changes
- Societal changes (large-scale changes in attitudes or behaviors)

Competitive Analysis

The SWOT analysis can be used not only to pinpoint your own situation but also that of your competition. You can begin by identifying your top three to five competitors by name. List each competitor's strengths and weaknesses in a chart format so comparisons can be made. Table 3.3 lists some of the items that might be included.

Marketing Objectives

Marketing objectives need to take into account the company's overall business plan. When looking at priorities, it is important to determine not only what actions are needed but also how these actions will be viewed by the plan's various partners, supporters, and beneficiaries, both inside and outside the company.

Clear and achievable objectives need to be established and communicated to all parties, including the rest of the marketing department, product development, management, the sales force, service areas, and any other group within the organization on which your plan can have an impact. Your objectives should be projected over a time

TABLE 3.3 Competitive Assessment

Assessment criteria	Our Company	Competitor A	Competitor B	Competitor C
Market share				
Estimated marketing budget ($)				
Estimated net sales ($)				
Size of sales force				
Unique selling advantage(s)				
Pricing (high/moderate/low)				
Target segments				
Brand awareness				

period—*x* percent over *y* years (see the example in Table 3.4). Here are some common objectives:

- To grow profits, revenues, or market share in a certain market
- To increase the number of customers
- To increase the proportion of customers who are highly profitable or otherwise valuable (for example, as referral sources)
- To increase the size of customer accounts or the amount of activity in those accounts
- To reposition a product
- To launch a new product/service enhancement
- To build brand awareness for long-term profitability
- To increase the number of products or services you cross-sell to current customers
- To increase retention rates
- To increase share of wallet

The marketing objectives for a local bank might look like Table 3.4.

Implementation

Before you develop tactics for meeting your objectives, you first need to determine your resources. What is your budget? How big is your staff? Will the plan be implemented by your own department or by others? How much authority do you have over those who will be charged with implementing your plan (such as an outside sales force)?

Budgets are usually outside the control of marketers; the funds available may be a percentage of sales or may be based on a formula derived from competitive analysis and marketing objectives—or, in the case of a small business, on how much cash is in the till. No marketer ever has enough money to do everything that is desired.

TABLE 3.4 Goals Should Be Specific and Measurable

	Current	1-year goal	2-year goal	3-year goal
Assets ($)				
Earnings ($)				
Average loan size ($)				
Average deposits ($)				
No. of deposit accounts				

Note: For each heading, you may also want to include percentage increase and rank versus competition estimates.

You'll hear the complaint from those with multimillion-dollar budgets and from those with no budgets at all. Budget will indeed determine what your marketing options are, but creative marketers can accomplish far more on a small budget than they think. Other steps in implementing the plan include the following:

Get buy-in from all concerned parties. Understand your management's and sales team's objectives and goals. Make a point of meeting with the management team to review the market plan and gain buy-in. Programs are more likely to be successful if management and sales input is solicited and incorporated.

Leverage partnerships. Take advantage of programs that may be available on a co-op basis or that are centrally managed and funded. Be alert to ways in which national advertising campaigns, corporate sponsorships, sales contests, and product launches can help you. Make sure these activities are integrated so local offices and branches are aware of the activities and can plan local events accordingly.

Establish a tracking and measurement process. A process must be put in place to capture the information and to provide the tools needed to track each program and measure success.

Continually evaluate all existing marketing programs and change or modify aspects that aren't working. The plan must be fluid and adapted to changing internal and external environments. Review progress at intervals short enough to catch developing problems early.

Assign responsibilities for implementation and tracking. The plan will not succeed unless all the people on the team know what they must do to execute the plan and measure the results.

Insure that your proposed tactics can be communicated to and executed by others. When implementing tactics over different geographic locations with different staffs, the plan must ensure that the tactics are replicable and cost effective. This may mean beta testing a tactic in one location and rolling it out across markets as results merit. If the size of the market and the cost of reaching the market vary from location to location, the plan should address how tactics will vary with those factors.

Communicate successes early and often. Establish a means to gather program feedback—best practices or lessons learned as well as hard numbers—and identify a vehicle to communicate this feedback to the sales force, management, and other partners. Communicate any early "wins" as soon as possible. It will set the right tone and provide some immediate support for the program.

Implementation Tactics

The universe of marketing communications tools is vast and ever-growing. Consider the tools outlined in Table 3.5 as you brainstorm possible tactics for your campaign. Chapters 4 through 11 discuss each of these tools in more detail.

TABLE 3.5 Selected Implementation Tools—A Checklist

Media Advertising
Radio
Television
Digital: banners, pay per click, contextual, and so on
Signage (outdoor, transit)
Co-op advertising
Print (newspapers; magazine, trade, and professional journals; advertorials; Yellow Pages; specialized directories and trade books)

Public Relations
Media and blogger relations
Media events
Public speaking
Bylined articles, blogs, and op-ed pieces

Event and Cause Sponsorship
Sponsorship of existing events (sporting, cultural, educational)
Cause marketing (working with a charitable group by donating a portion of sales, providing goods or services, or underwriting and publicizing events)
"Activation" events associated with a sponsorship, including contests, giveaways, special events

Interactive Marketing
Mail campaigns
Online campaigns
On-site or guerilla campaigns (such as product sampling)
Mobile Marketing including app development
Microsites for products or client segments
Intranet or other limited-access web sites
Content marketing campaigns
Social media campaigns

Personal Selling
Lead-generation campaigns
Personalized letters, calls, and meetings
Customized proposals
Presentation/sales materials
Sales training
Sales contests
Exhibiting at trade shows and industry events
Holding seminars for prospects and clients
Convened events, such as panels, symposia, and round tables

Relationship Marketing
Retention-marketing programs (special programs for new customers, loyalty programs)
Cross-sell and up-sell programs
Referral marketing
Customer publications

Choosing Tactics

Given the large number of potential tactics, how does a marketer choose which to implement? From a strategic standpoint, the answers should be based on a combination of factors:

Selected client characteristics. What web sites do they visit, watch, do for entertainment? What is the most effective way to reach them? How do they like to be contacted (in-person, mail, online, phone)?

Opportunities in the marketplace. Are there special events that lend themselves to a seminar? For example, are there tax changes your clients should know about?

Competitive behavior. Are your competitors advertising heavily? Have competitors entered or exited your markets?

Short- and long-term objectives. Are you trying to generate leads for your sales force or outright sales? Are you trying to build brand awareness for the long term or generate a "quick hit"?

Budget. Although marketing dollars and staff resources shouldn't be the first consideration in tactical planning, budget will certainly have a major impact on what you can do. But bear in mind that no budget ever seems big enough. Effective planning, creativity and resourcefulness are more important than dollars.

Even with identical budgets, two companies will likely come up with different tactical marketing plans. There is no formula for choosing marketing tactics. However, the matrix in Table 3.6 can provide a starting point for prioritizing tactical decisions.

Metrics to Track and Measure Success

Tracking and measuring marketing programs can be a challenge. Depending on the nature of the program, anecdotal results may be the best that can be hoped for—an ad that gets a salesperson an appointment, which in turn leads to a big sale; positive client feedback on a new loyalty membership benefit; or good press from a new corporate sponsorship event. Although these results can and should be shared with top management, there will be disappointment that they are not definitively quantifiable.

Senior management is increasingly demanding accountability for marketing dollars. "Track and measure" is a corporate mantra forcing marketers to demonstrate the value and return of a program, through a payback analysis or calculation of return on investment (ROI). Management consultant Peter Drucker is attributed with the expression, "If you can't measure it you can't manage it." Others have adapted the phrase, claiming, "if you can't measure it, it doesn't exist." For marketers the ability to measure the use and relative success of each dollar plays an important role in building or ending careers.

TABLE 3.6 Choosing Tactics

Advantages	Disadvantages	Resources usage	Objective
Display Advertising			
Depending on vehicle selected, can reach mass audiences or highly targeted ones. Cost per thousand (CPM) is low.	Cost per prospect is often relatively high. No definitive way to measure effectiveness.	Costs range from moderate to high. For most organizations, ad specialists are outsourced.	Awareness building. Branding. Retention marketing.
Public relations			
If successful, powerful "third-party endorsement" has higher credibility than advertising.	No control over whether message appears or in what context.	Relatively low cost. Can be done with limited staff or outsourced expertise.	Awareness and brand building. Establishing name in the marketplace. Relationship building.
Sponsorships			
Opportunity to associate brand name with event or cause favored by target markets. Exclusive venue for sales team to meet with clients and prospects. Opportunities to motivate internal staff.	Sales effectiveness not easily measurable. Must be planned carefully to achieve goals.	Sponsorship costs can be low or high, but activation will cost an additional 50 to 150%. Need for large staff resources.	Awareness building. Lead generation. Relationship building.
Interactive Marketing			
Highly targeted. Results easily measured.	Can create negative image (junk messaging, spam, apps that crash).	Low on a cost-per-contact basis. High on CPM basis. Usually outsourced.	Sales. Sales leads. Relationship building.
Social Media			
Establish reputation for expertise. Employ wisdom of crowds. Build fan base.	Difficult to control. Threats to brand. Need to respond rapidly.	Cost varies. Design and programming are usually outsourced. High time commitment.	Sales. Sales leads. Image building. Relationship building.
Personal Selling			
Most personal method. Measurable results.	Highest cost. Results vary by skill and experience of sales person.	High.	Sales. Sales leads. Image building. Relationship building.
Trade Shows and Seminars			
One-on-one opportunity to demonstrate expertise.	Only as good as the people who work them.	Variable. Trade shows need sufficient staff resources.	Sales leads. Image building. Relationship building.
Relationship Marketing			
Most profitable return on marketing dollars.	Difficult to do well.	Variable.	Retention. Referrals. Cross-sell. Up-sell.

Financial Services Lag in Measuring Return on Marketing Investment (ROMI)

According to an invaluable 2007 study by consulting firm Booz & Company "financial services companies have thus far made less progress" in unlocking the value of return on investment (ROI) measurements "than companies in other industries."

While the top 10 U.S. financial services companies spend more than 3.6 percent of their revenue on marketing, "FS companies struggle to identify business results that can be directly attributed to marketing actions...The paradox of FS marketing is that the industry has access to more marketing data than nearly any other industry, but it is much more difficult to capture, analyze, and act on this data."

Where marketing return is measured, results may vary depending on what is measured, how it is measured and the specific campaign variables. In one study cited by Booz & Company, the ROI for a single bank varied from +410% to −100%. (In other words, the company lost a dollar on each dollar spent.)

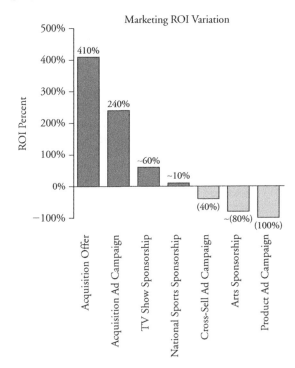

Marketing ROI Variation

Source: Booz & Company, 2007

Among the recommendations offered by the Booz & Company study are the following:

Establish a Base Level of Sales. Using regression modeling tools, establish the relative weight of all variables that can have an impact, such as seasonal variations or macroeconomic changes, such as rising interest rates. Then develop a formula to set the comparative pre-campaign sales baseline. These variables should be filtered out of the regression model. The objective during this stage is to figure out how to isolate the marketing campaign, by peeling away external or environmental impact.

Determine Sales Lift. Using the same model, examine coefficients on marketing variables to estimate the impact of the initiative on sales—that is, the number of incremental products sold directly attributable to the marketing campaign. The process is refined over time: Insignificant variables are discarded, questionable variables examined further.

Determine lifetime value. To determine the lifetime value of the customer, use a formula that includes elements such as the annual discount rate, the average tenure of a customer with a particular product, and the pretax annual profit per product sold.

Calculate ROI. Multiply the number of products sold (sales lift) by the lifetime value figure. Divide by the marketing cost to calculate ROI.

Source: Climbing the Learning Curve: Understanding Marketing ROI in Financial Services. Booz & Company, 2007. Used with permission. http://www.booz.com/global/home/what_we_think/reports_and_white_papers/ic-display/41901746

The Limits of Measurement

Some tactical programs are easy to measure. Direct response through mail, phone, or e-mail usually yields hard sales numbers and an immediate calculation of ROI. Some tactics are measurable over time, like relationship-building and loyalty programs that are designed to increase retention and cross-sell. These can be measured against a control group or against earlier retention and cross-sell rates.

Then there are programs that involve direct, one-to-one selling. The problem here is not a lack of data but the difficulty of gathering the data. It is notoriously difficult to get salespeople to fill out tracking reports, although this problem is beginning to abate as producer optimization systems automatically track contact and sales data. Programs that involve the sales force—whether at trade shows, seminars, or in face-to-face selling—can be measured, provided the data are tracked.

The most difficult types of tactics to track and measure are advertising, public relations, event sponsorship, and other programs where sales are not directly attributable to the promotion. If the campaigns are designed to build awareness, proxy measures—such as number of ad views, recall scores, and media placements—can measure success. But the reliable correlation of increased sales (if any) to an advertising or public relations campaign is a problem still looking for a resolution.

The problem may not be a lack of data so much as a lack of access to the data. The ability to track and measure activity is not solely the responsibility of the marketing department. Rather, it requires a corporate-wide commitment and the cooperation of management, marketing, operations, information technology (IT), service, sales, and product management.

What to Measure

Before rushing off to create a tracking process, an extremely important question needs to be asked: What needs to be tracked? For many, the answer will be sales. However, along the road to tracking sales there is a wide array of information that can also be obtained. For a trade show, for example, measurement data might include attendance numbers, clients and prospects in attendance, demographic information, sales leads, brand impressions, appointments made, cost per lead or sale, and lifetime value of customers. What can be measured is limited only by cost and the thought and planning required to set up the infrastructure.

Market Planning Checklist

Like a last-minute check of your tires before you go on a trip, Table 3.7 can help make sure you've thought of everything. When you are comfortable with the answers to these questions, you are ready to implement your market plan.

TABLE 3.7   *Marketing Plan Checklist*

What is the business reason for this strategy or program? Simply put, why is this program important?

What are the specific objectives?

By what variables will success be measured?

Is the budget sufficient? If not, what programs stay or go?

Is the program sustainable and can it be replicated?

Is there buy-in from management, the sales force, the marketing team, and the necessary support groups?

Is Compliance aware of the marketing material and/or product being created?

Do all the right people understand the objective?

How does this market plan fit into the company's overall priorities?

What needs to be done to implement the market plan to achieve the company's expected results?

Is product training needed?

Is collateral material available?

Have goals been established and communicated?

Have the necessary tracking and measurement tools been put into place?

Marketing Tactics

CHAPTER 4

Advertising

To most people, advertising *is* marketing. It is often the first tactic to come to mind when a sales or product manager is seeking to build sales. But media advertising (as opposed to direct marketing, online or digital marketing, and tactics discussed in other chapters) is just one element in the marketing mix. There are many reasons to use media advertising—whether print, broadcast, online, outdoor, or mobile.

These are among media advertising's most important functions:

- *Brand building.* This is the main reason most companies use brand or "image" advertising (that is, advertising not specifically designed to sell a particular product). Keep in mind that most financial services are bought irregularly. Buyers pay little attention to advertising for products or services that they are not looking to buy. Therefore, the task of financial advertising is to generate a sufficient level of awareness over time to be "top of mind" when the buyer is ready, say, to take out a mortgage, finance a new business, establish an IRA, or engage a new investment banker.
- *Familiarity.* Advertising gives potential buyers the comfort that they are making the right decision. It is easier for someone to buy from a company that is well known than to take a chance on an unknown quantity. This familiarity also "softens the beaches" for the sales force.
- *Customer retention.* Advertising reinforces satisfaction among those who have already purchased from a company. In a proprietary study conducted by a leading brokerage firm, advertising was found to have little measurable impact on acquisition of new customers but had a significant effect on client retention.
- *Reaching third-party influencers.* Institutional advertising is often aimed at senior management rather than at those who actually buy a particular product, with the aim of getting a "trickle-down" referral from the top. Similarly, financial advisers are more comfortable recommending products they feel are well-known to the public.
- *Maintaining market share.* Companies may be forced into "defensive advertising" in order to keep up with their competitors' ad expenditures and avoid losing market share.
- *Improving employee morale.* Advertising can have a positive effect on staff motivation and make recruitment easier.

Media Selection

Which advertising media should carry one's advertising message? All of them. Assuming you've got the money, each channel reinforces the others and reaches target segments in different ways. A successful campaign may use print and broadcast coupled with online channels, to create the strongest possible impact.

Ally Bank needed to establish a brand virtually overnight. The bank grew out of GMAC (General Motors' financing arm), but was launched as a separate brand in 2009. By mid-2010, Ally had spent $121 million on broadcast, print, and online advertising. As a result, 97 percent of those polled had awareness of the brand.[1]

The value of message integration across channels is particularly important considering that even television is viewed on more than just television sets. Consumers are watching via the Internet and on mobile devices, in-home and out-of-home, live and time-shifted, free and paid, rebroadcast and original programs. Advertising has followed viewers to online videos, online TV shows, TV show sponsorship, branded entertainment, online streaming, video on mobile phones, and more.

According to eMarketer.com, ad formats such as banner ads, sponsorships, and video ads are all growing even faster than paid search. In 2011, video ad spending grew by more than 50 percent, sponsorship by 25 percent, banner ads by 22 percent, and search by 20 percent. By 2015 online display-ad spending is predicted to surpass paid search.

As with any marketing decision, your choice of where to advertise is a function of target segments, objectives, and budget. It might appear obvious to use online and mobile media if your target market is young. But these are also important tactics if you are aiming at institutional buyers, such as financial advisors or pension consultants. If your objective is to deliver sales leads, then print and online may be your most

---

Multiple Advertising Media Drive Online Response

While paid search is an important element in overall advertising effectiveness, the most successful campaigns employ multiple media. American Family Insurance created a multi-media approach to build their "Trusted Advice" campaign, including radio, an online branded entertainment series *(In Gayle We Trust)*, and a micro-site, "Building a Better Future," for the educational portion of the campaign.

Traffic from all three channels pointed back to American Family Insurance's web site. As a result of the campaign, American Family Insurance saw:

1. A double-digit increase in web visitors.
2. A triple-digit increase in web traffic.
3. A triple-digit increase in online quote activity.
4. A double-digit increase in time spent on the site.

Source: "American Family Insurance: A Case for Multi-Screen Marketing." ANA 2011 TV & Everything Video Forum, 02/10/11; Digital, Social, and Mobile Members Only Conference, 03/02/11.

effective choices. Television is fine if you have a big budget or if you have a regional market that can be reached efficiently through local broadcasters or cable stations.

Print Advertising

The complexity of financial products lends itself to the written word. Whereas video is particularly adept at conveying emotions, words are better able to communicate facts and figures.

Print advertising includes newspapers, consumer magazines, specialized trade magazines, and directories (everything from the Yellow Pages to specialized industry directories). Most print publications now have online versions.

When deciding on advertising in print publications and related web sites, consider which publications your target markets read. Media selection is somewhat simpler on the institutional side, as there are standard trade journals that everyone in a given industry reads (for example, in investment management and retirement planning, such publications as *Institutional Investor* and *Pensions & Investments*). On the consumer side, media placement is more complex and a highly specialized subject. Ad agencies, digital agencies, and specialized media firms perform sophisticated analyses to determine which of thousands of media opportunities best match target market segments.

How much can you afford to spend? Print ads, depending on their size and the circulation of the publication, can range from several hundred dollars—for a local daily or weekly publication with a circulation of several thousand—to upward of $200,000 for a full-page ad in the *Wall Street Journal*.

It is important to keep in mind that advertising page rates will vary greatly depending on whether the ad is black-and-white or color, the overall bargaining power of the advertiser, the number of pages and repeats being contracted for, and whether the ad will appear in regional or national editions. Bargains can sometimes be found by waiting until the last minute for left-over space in a publication.

Another consideration is where your competitors are advertising. During the market boom of the 1990s, ads from mutual fund companies fattened consumer financial titles like *Money*, *Smart Money*, and *Kiplinger's*. But with so many companies advertising the same type of product, the message got lost in the clutter. Smart advertisers began looking for alternatives, like shelter magazines and other publications aimed at wealthy consumers.

The Role of Your Ad Agency

Any company with enough money to buy advertising should use an agency to create and place the ads. Some companies will also ask their agencies to handle strategic assignments, such as identifying target markets and the appropriate media for reaching them.

The agency will help you determine, given your budget, where you can expect the greatest return for your investment in ad dollars. Selecting an advertising agency is

---

Don't Overlook Radio

Too many advertisers forget about radio, but in many markets, radio reaches more people than many other media. Depending on the time slot, radio has these additional advantages:

It's inexpensive. Radio spots often cost less than print or online for equivalent cost-per-thousand (CPM) prospects. What's more, radio ads are not expensive to produce—if you want, you can just provide a script, and the radio announcer will read it.

It's clutter-free. People don't zap radio ads the way they do television. Listening to the radio may be the only thing that people in a car are doing other than driving, so you have a very large share of their attention.

It's targetable. In many markets, some radio stations may be reaching small ethnic and other communities that may otherwise be difficult to access. A financial adviser of West Indian background had considerable success using a radio station directed at Caribbean audiences for advertising and related publicity.

---

often a complicated job that may require hiring a consultant to prepare the request for proposal (RFP) and help in the evaluation and selection process. The steps that follow have been adapted from the publication *Selecting an Advertising Agency*, published by the Association of National Advertisers.

Develop an agency "job description."
- Identify the functions the agency will perform, such as account service, research, and media buying and the specific types of assignments, such as new product introductions, positioning or repositioning, brand building.
- Determine whether the assignment will be local, regional, national, or global.
- Will the agency be joining a roster of other agencies, or will there be an exclusive arrangement?
- With which departments and outside vendors (such as PR) will the agency need to coordinate?
- What industry expertise is expected (i.e., does the agency's financial services background need to be strong in retail or institutional, banking or investments?).

Determine what size agency is desirable.
A smaller agency will dedicate its top people to an account that a large agency might assign to junior or less experienced staff. On the other hand, the larger the agency, the deeper and broader its resources.

Consider potential conflicts.
Conflicts are a matter of judgment. A competitor can be either broadly defined as any financial services provider (whether involved in banking,

insurance, credit, or investments) or more narrowly defined to include only directly competing product lines. Or conflict can be limited, based on the marketplace the company serves. For example, a Chicago regional bank might not object to its agency handling a similar regional bank in San Francisco, as long as their markets didn't overlap.

Narrow the list of potential agencies.

After you have reduced the candidates to a small group, issue an RFP seeking more information about the agency's experience, size, client list, personnel, and other matters of interest. From the questionnaire, and any personal interviews, you will generally narrow the choice down to two or three firms. If you have the budget, you can commission each of the finalists to prepare a sample ad. Do not expect an agency to do it "on spec" (that is, without compensation).

Creating Effective Creative

The classic theory of advertising is that it is based on awareness, interest, desire, and action (AIDA). First you have to get the target's attention; then you have to provide a reason to listen to your message; the message needs to stimulate the desire for the

---

Selecting an Agency

During the financial crisis of 2008, Morgan Stanley looked like it was near collapse. The aspirational creative messaging that had been created in 2007 was no longer setting an appropriate tone for the brand.

In 2007, Morgan Stanley had acquired Smith Barney, creating a giant global wealth-management firm. Morgan Stanley sought to create a campaign for the new firm, emphasizing new leadership in wealth management. With the change in both the firm's role and the global economic crisis, Morgan Stanley put its advertising out for review. Its objectives were to:

- Restore the mystique of the Morgan Stanley brand.
- Integrate the cultures of Morgan Stanley and Smith Barney.

A four-person internal team conducted the search. "We selected The Martin Agency based on three factors: first, their experience and track record in financial services; second, their understanding of our strategy; and third, their ability to execute highly creative advertising that will help define and differentiate our brand," said Morgan Stanley's chief marketing officer.

Source: "Agency Transition in a Time of Transition." ANA, 03/08/11 and http://www.adweek.com/news/advertising-branding/morgan-stanley-picks-martin-agency-107120

product; and finally, the target needs to buy whatever it is you are selling. While overly simplistic, the AIDA model has some element of truth.

Effective creative (copy and art) should perform the first three of the AIDA functions—get noticed in a cluttered environment, be interesting, and establish a reason to buy—or at least to think of the brand the next time a potential customer is in the market for the product. Online, the loop may be closed, although it is likely that an online viewer will still need some interaction with a live sales person (through an online or phone conversation) before purchasing. Action is usually dependent on point-of-purchase information, often supplied by the salesperson.

Institutional Advertising Doesn't Have to Be Dull

The client, a not-for-profit cooperative that provides retirement plans for banks and credit unions, was a preferred provider for an association of national credit unions. It developed an online ad for the association's web site that featured a premium of a white paper comparing retirement plans for those who clicked on the ad.

How does your retirement plan stack up?

Are your retirement plan benefits giving you all the value you and your employees deserve?

Download the FREE white paper, "Retirement Planning Checklist for credit Unions."

Retirement isn't about plans, it's about people.

Will your employees have enough to retire on? Will you?

Both of these approaches focus on benefits to the credit union and use a free white paper to drive action. The pancake imagery is probably more attention getting, but the people photos may be more relevant to the copy.

Effective advertising communicates quickly. The average person takes less than 30 seconds to look at a print ad (and less for an online display ad), and very few ads are noticed at all. In print and online, the headline alone should tell the whole story, mentioning both the product and the key benefit. For example, consider a Fidelity Investments ad headlined: "Want to make sure your plan is on track? Fidelity can help." It's not brilliantly creative, but it is perfectly pitched to a target worried about losing money in a down market.

Making the Most of the Headline and Visual

The two most critical elements in a print or online ad are the headline and the visual (photo or other illustration). If neither the headline nor the visual attracts the reader's attention, it is likely the ad will be overlooked. The headline and graphic need to do all of the following: appeal specifically to the target market, describe a need or benefit, and arouse curiosity or in some way disturb the reader so the message is read.

Below are a few tips for making sure print advertising is noticed, read, and serves your objectives, based on classic advice from David Ogilvy. Much of this advice applies to online display advertising as well.

- Always use headlines and an illustration.
- Relate the illustration to the headline. Otherwise it may be misunderstood.
- Photos do a better job of attracting a reader's attention than drawings.
- Before-and-after photos are effective. So are babies (think eTrade) and animals (i.e., Merrill Lynch's bull, Pacific Life's whale, AXA-Equitable's gorilla, MetLife's Snoopy) and sex, though the last is probably not appropriate for most financial ads. Many financial ads show "aspirational" images, such as luxurious settings, romantic retirement travel, and well-heeled clients whose finances seem to be well looked-after.
- Celebrities or well-known individuals will increase recognition and recall. Spokespeople do not have to be movie stars. Steve Martin was a less effective spokesman for Merrill Lynch than former superstar money manager Peter Lynch was for Fidelity, even though Martin is better known. The Fidelity ads with Peter Lynch were effective because he was known to the target market and was closely related to the company and its message.
- Avoid negative words in a headline (no, not, nothing, none). Readers skip over them and may associate the product with a negative quality.
- Don't be afraid of long copy. If the target is interested, more information is better than less. When using long copy, break up the copy with bullet points, numbers, or graphic elements.
- Use a call to action—a phone number or web site—so the reader can act on any interest the ad has created.
- Don't make ads difficult to read. Keep layouts simple. Do not use reverse type (white on black). Avoid sans serif type except in headlines. Avoid justified type with a rigid right-hand margin—or worse, centered type—for body copy. Always make headlines in upper and lower case. If the targets can't read the ad easily, they won't.

What's Wrong with This Ad?

Although this advertiser has only seconds to grab attention, it will take the target that long just to figure out how to read the headline, much less comprehend it. This is an art director's ad—pretty, but difficult to read. The headline is all caps, the body copy is in reverse, sans serif type, justified.

The good news is that the illustration is dramatic and eye-catching. Readers might stop long enough to look at the picture—but what will they take away from the headline? The brand name is not mentioned. There is no benefit beyond a vague claim that client companies (nature unspecified) are helped to seize opportunities of some kind. For the advertiser, an opportunity has been wasted.

What Makes Good Creative?

The Financial Communications Society has sponsored the annual Portfolio awards for best financial advertising since 1994. When asked, "What makes great creative?" Bill Wreaks, past president of the society and publisher of the *Journal of Financial Advertising & Marketing*, looks for "creative messaging that is relevant, resonant, and simple." Veteran graphic designer Piet Halberstadt asks, "Does it enhance the product and inform the viewer?" Bob Kuperman, former president of DDB Needham, also thinks simplicity is the key to notable financial advertising, although, as Mark Dimassimo,

Creativity That Sells

The number of creative awards a campaign wins is usually not a good measure of strategic effectiveness. But solid creative input that generates attention, is memorable, is well liked, and serves strategic ends, can lead to synergies that multiply the effectiveness of a campaign. A good example is MasterCard's "Priceless" campaign.

Until 1997, MasterCard was regarded in the marketplace as the "other" card—one with no strong product differentiation. Five different brand campaigns in less than a dozen years and 15 different agency partners globally were, in part, responsible for this muddy brand image. Following rigorous consumer research and an agency review, MasterCard picked McCann-Erickson, which devised the "priceless" campaign with its tag line: "There are some things money can't buy. For everything else, there's MasterCard." Not only did the concept test well with consumers in the United States, but it was also a winner in every global market tested. The campaign has been used in more than 90 countries in more than 45 languages.

MasterCard's "Priceless" campaign debuted in 1997 and increased purchase volume by 64 percent over the next five years. The number of MasterCard–branded cards increased by more than 52 percent over the same time period, driving six times more volume than anything the company had done before.

The campaign's adaptability has been key to its success. Integrated marketing programs and promotions—including sports sponsorships, online contests, even an iPhone "Priceless Picks" app—multiply the campaign's effectiveness. MasterCard has adapted the campaign for local markets, not just internationally but also regionally within the United States.

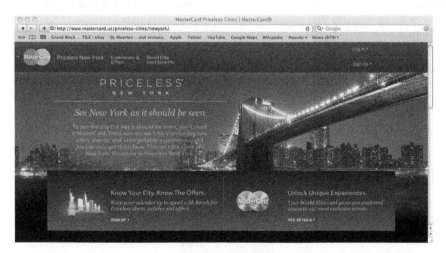

The success of the creative component has given MasterCard another advantage: cultural currency. "Priceless" has become one of very few ad campaigns to become part of popular culture—referred to on everything from Comedy Central to Jay Leno, parodies on YouTube, even web sites devoted to "priceless" jokes.

Source: "The Power of the Brand," *The Advertiser* (Association of National Advertisers), October 2002.

CEO and creative director of Dimassimo Goldstein points out, "a lot of simple campaigns out there are simply awful."

The long-running MasterCard "Priceless" campaign created by McCann Erickson, demonstrates the qualities of a multiple FCS Portfolio winner. Both simple and informative, it also contains an element often missing from financial advertising—emotion. Said Kuperman, "financial advertising does not have to be dry and devoid of emotion . . . [Good advertising] connects with emotions of what really matters in life."[2]

The Big Idea

When TD Bank North acquired Commerce Bank, it launched a campaign for the new brand, TD Bank. While renaming the bank, the merged company kept Commerce Bank's agency, its spokespeople, and its tagline: "America's Most Convenient Bank." The big idea for TD Bank was convenience.

To launch the campaign, TD Bank leveraged the convenience theme by providing more than a million free services. The campaign included a sweepstakes, *"At Your Convenience"* with prizes of a personal chef, chauffeur, or house cleaner. *"Random Acts of Convenience"* took the campaign to the streets—thousands of people were handed a free cup of coffee or an umbrella on a rainy day. Mall shoppers were offered free gift wrapping, courtesy of TD Bank. In partnership with local pizzerias and laundries, TD Bank delivered free pizzas and laundry services. "We tried to explore things that were convenient," a representative with Tierney Communications, TD Bank's ad agency said. "We're doing anything that makes people's lives more convenient."

Brand ads in newspaper and outdoor emphasized TD conveniences like seven-day banking, extended hours, free coin counting, free lollipops and doggie treats. TV and radio ads featured spokespeople Regis Philbin and Kelly Ripa in a humorous take on the convenience theme. Online ads were added, featuring animated versions of Regis and Kelly.

While TD Bank's campaign is beyond the budgets of most advertisers, it is a model of consistency and brand integration across marketing channels.

Source: "Merged Banks Use Guerilla Tactics to Launch New Brand," *The Financial Brand,* December 9, 2008.

The Creative Brief

It is important to have an unambiguous understanding of goals before creative work begins. One way is to collaborate on a "creative brief," that makes sure agencies and internal clients are on the same page.

The brief should clearly and succinctly (usually in two to three pages) spell out the purpose of the work and the key benefits that need to be communicated.

- What is the marketing challenge or objective of the creative?
- What's your point of difference? Is it functional or emotional?
- Who is the decision-maker for your product or service? What will appeal to them, not just intellectually but emotionally?
- What are the main benefits for this decision-maker?
- Proof points for the key benefits.
- Tonality and brand character.
- What is the big idea or unique selling proposition?

Measuring Advertising Effectiveness

Advertising that generates brand awareness may take years to pay off in actual sales, and the connection between the two may never be measurable.

The impact of advertising on sales is notoriously difficult to measure, as it is difficult to isolate the effect of the advertising from all the other variables that impact sales. Nevertheless, there are qualitative and quantitative measures advertisers can apply to determine whether advertising is meeting its short- and long-term goals.

Qualitative measures include whether an ad is noticed and whether it is recalled, aided or unaided. Attitudinal changes toward the product or advertiser can also be measured through focus groups, interviews, and surveys.

Quantitative measures of effectiveness include:

- Number of inquiries or sales directly attributable to the campaign.
- Variations from comparable periods in market share; size of customer base; purchase frequency; average size of purchase; percentage of total assets held ("wallet share"); and profitability and length of customer tenure (lifetime value).
- Test campaigns against a control (or in spot markets).
- The effect of a campaign can also be measured using multivariate regression analysis. This statistical technique examines the relationships between one dependent variable (sales, for example) and multiple independent variables (for example, the individual elements of the marketing mix). This enables marketers to estimate the relative importance of each of the independent variables and to compare the financial return from each of the various inputs with its dollar cost.

Clearly, advertising pays off in increased sales or advertisers wouldn't bother running the ads. As proof, the Internet offers an opportunity to compare paid search ads against natural search. In 2010, for example, Bank of America (BofA) had a daily Google AdWords budget ranging from $22,160 to $95,910. BofA used 30,465 keywords, which resulted in some 56,800 paid clicks. The bank's organic search resulted in 122,000 clicks.[3] Why bother spending on paid search if free search led to more clicks? Studies have shown that "conversion rates, order values, and profits from paid search advertisements are much higher than those from natural search."[4]

Legal and Regulatory Considerations

After pharmaceuticals, financial services are probably the most highly regulated of all industries when it comes to advertising. Like all advertisers, financial services companies must comply with general advertising guidelines prohibiting advertising that is untruthful, deceptive, or unfair. But financial advertisers have many additional regulatory requirements—mandated by the federal government (such as the Federal Trade Commission [FTC] and the Securities and Exchange Commission [SEC]), industry associations (such as the Financial Industry Regulatory Authority [FINRA]), and various departments within each individual state (state banking department, attorney general's office, insurance office). In fact, financial services may be the only industry in which some advertising is prohibited altogether: for example, the SEC has fined hedge funds that advertise in consumer publications.

What can happen if a financial services firm runs afoul of these laws? Fines, substantial penalties, and potential lawsuits. For example, a bank was sued under the federal Truth in Lending Act for advertising "no annual fee," and then charging such a fee six months later. The court ruled against the bank, despite other language in the ads giving it the right to change terms.

For marketers, the severity of regulation means a lot of small print in advertising. (But not too small—Rule 420(a) of the Securities Act mandates that all copy, including footnotes, be in "roman type at least as large and as legible as 8-point modern type.") It also means reviews by legal and compliance officers, sending marketing copy to Washington, D.C., for preapproval, and generally a lot of interference with what the "creatives" want to do. This is not to mention a whole new regulatory can of worms opened by the social media, which is addressed in Chapter 8.

Field Advertising and Co-op Programs

Financial companies with field offices usually offer funding to their sales forces to offset the cost of local advertising. The objectives of the advertising programs vary, but most focus on building prospects' awareness of the local office.

Co-op advertising allows the salesperson to share the cost of the advertising with headquarters. Companies that use co-op advertising usually create preapproved ads that can be personalized with names and/or photos.

Some companies offer programs that allow salespeople to create their own ads as long as compliance and branding guidelines are followed. Generally, these are monitored to ensure correct and approved usage.

Conclusion

In the Internet age, advertising is more important than ever for marketers and their audiences. Advertising helps the marketer get its name and product known to its markets. Advertising gives potential buyers an assurance that they are making good decisions by offering them a well-known name. Combined with other media, advertising can open markets, help acquire customers, and reinforce purchase decisions.

Notes

1. "If Advertising Doesn't Work, Then Why is 'Ally' a Household Word?", *The Financial Brand*, November 12, 2010.
2. Bill Wreaks interview with all individuals quoted, February 2004.
3. "Spy on your AdWords Competitors with SpyFu," *The Financial Brand*, September 14, 2010.
4. Anindya Ghose and Sha Yang, "Comparing Performance Metrics in Organic Search with Sponsored Search Advertising," http://pages.stern.nyu.edu/~aghose/organic_sponsored.pdf

CHAPTER 5

Public Relations

If you asked a group of consumers or even professionals to define public relations (PR), you invariably would hear it described as "free advertising." This is not a good definition because PR isn't advertising, and it isn't free. Rather, public relations is a means of positioning your products or company through a perceived third-party endorsement.

How much of financial services advertising that you see or read each day do you act on? When was the last time you discussed a financial ad with a friend or colleague? Now, consider your reaction to a recent news story or post—whether print, television, or online—concerning the financial industry. How much of your attention did it receive? Did you discuss it with a friend or colleague? It is likely that you spent more time thinking about the news story than the advertisement. That is also the bottom line when comparing advertising with public relations.

Too many marketers, particularly in financial services, give short shrift to public relations as a tactic for image building for their company or product. Public relations is one of the most effective means of shaping attitudes and building credibility for you, your organization, and its products.

With the rise of the social web, the definition of public relations has expanded. This chapter will look beyond what used to be called "ink"—that is, mentions in an article or column by a professional journalist. Today's influencers are no longer exclusively traditional journalists. Bloggers have grown increasingly important to getting the word out, as have "consumer journalists." Comments on news sites may have as much influence as the original story. Twitter posts can send an item viral with a speed unimagined in the days when newspapers and television were the main source of most information.

While the media have changed, the principles of good public relations remain the same. Additional insights into influencing group-sourced, non-professional social media, such as LinkedIn or Yelp, can be found in Chapter 8, Social Media Marketing.

PR encompasses a wide variety of disciplines, including investor relations, crisis management, internal communications, influencing government policy, and community relations. This chapter will look primarily at PR as a marketing tactic—that is, how to use public relations to achieve your marketing objectives.

Third-Party Endorsement

When an outside source lends you or your company credibility, you have received a third-party endorsement. It could be inclusion in a magazine list of the best local banks for service or a blog post citing an example of your company's outstanding service. It could be an article you wrote, under your own byline, demonstrating your expertise on a particular subject which appears in a trade magazine or local newspaper. It could be a quotation attributed to you by a reporter who interviewed you as a source for a story. It might be a presentation you make at a professional conference. By selecting you as a speaker, the organization is, in effect, acknowledging your skills and abilities. It is the third-party, presumably objective, nature of this endorsement that brings you and your organization believability.

Consider the difference in impact between announcing something yourself and having a third party say the same thing about you. When you tell people "I just received a major industry award," or "the company just landed a major client," whether in person or through advertising, it is perceived as puffery. When someone else says or writes something about the same event, it has far more credibility.

PR is not better than advertising—it's different (see Table 5.1). One key difference is that you cannot control what is written or broadcast about you or your company. An editor may reject your press release as too self-serving or lacking in interest to readers, members, or viewers. Conversely, the story idea you pitch may turn out to be of tremendous interest to a reporter, but you may see little, if anything, about your company in the finished piece.

On the web you have even less control. Anyone with a computer can denigrate your product or make untrue statements that reflect badly on your company. That's why it is even more important now than in the past to be proactive about protecting and projecting your image in a positive way.

Getting positive press is the most effective way to create favorable public opinion. By directing your message to the audiences you want to reach, your goals are to generate positive feelings toward your firm, differentiate the company from its competitors, and help position the company in the marketplace.

TABLE 5.1   Advertising versus Public Relations

	Advertising	Public Relations
Cost	High to moderate	Moderate to low
Objective	Build/maintain awareness	Establish credibility and build awareness
Placement	Advertiser chooses time and place	Editor or publisher decides where and whether to include
Who controls the message?	Advertiser	Editor or publisher
Market perception	Puffery	Objective third-party endorsement

The Tarnished Image of Financial Services

Let's face it. Bankers have replaced communists as Hollywood's favorite villains. Bankers are behind international conspiracies in movies from *Wall Street* to *The International*. At the height of the financial crisis in 2008, only 20 percent of Americans trusted America's financial system, according to a survey by the Kellogg School of Management at Northwestern University, a number that has not improved in recent years. The 2011 survey showed trust in banks was 32 percent, in mutual funds 25 percent, and in the stock market 12 percent.

As a sector whose livelihood depends on its customers' trust, financial services clearly needs to repair its image on a major scale.

Source: http://www.loansafe.org/financial-trust-index-overall-trust-in-americas-financial-system-stumbles-to-20

The Tools of Public Relations

The classic PR tool is the press release or press kit. A press release is a structured document. It is written like a news story, beginning with the headline. The headline should convey something newsworthy or something contrary to expectations, and must serve your objective. "Barracuda Bank to Take Over Local Small Bank" is a newsworthy headline for a local paper, but probably puts the wrong spin on the acquisition if you're writing for Barracuda. A better headline might be "[Name of Town] to Get Big-City Banking Benefits."

The press release continues in newspaper style, with the most important points of the story coming in the first paragraph. The second paragraph often contains a quote from one of those involved in the story. The idea is to make it simple for an editor to use your release as it is written. If the editor has space for only two paragraphs, make sure your first two paragraphs are the ones that get printed.

The traditional press kit provides additional information. It can be e-mailed, distributed during a press conference or event, or given personally to a reporter. A press kit may contain any or all of the following:

- Press releases
- Backgrounders or fact sheets about the company or product
- White papers about industry or issues of importance
- Biographies and photographs of the principals
- Suggested interview questions, with sample answers
- Brochures, newsletters, and other marketing material
- Links to web sites that reporters can refer to for more information

If possible, it is a good idea to include illustrations in your press kit. Videos can be posted to YouTube or your web site to encourage links from other sites. Media content generators look for visuals to illustrate a story, and they may be more likely to pay attention to the information if it comes with a photo, video, or even a slide, chart, graph, or other relevant piece of artwork.

Traditional press releases are still sent but the Internet has changed the traditional model. Today's news distributors are no longer dependent on press releases to find information and sources. According to a 2008 survey, 91 percent of journalists use search engines to research companies, find media experts and learn about past media coverage. An additional large percentage use social networks, blogs, and Wikis to find news sources.[1]

SEO Press Releases

As online search has replaced informal networking as a way for reporters to find sources, the importance of search engine optimization (SEO) for press releases has grown. Keywords and links need to be identified and used across channels. Keywords should identify who you are and lead others to you. Links also raise your visibility on search engines.

Once you have identified the important keywords some best practices include:

- Use keywords in headlines, subheads, and opening paragraphs
- Use links from and to your release to all relevant sites, such as your YouTube postings, Twitter posts, and, of course, to your web site or blog
- Archive online media links with social bookmarking services, such as digg.com.

Note that keywords should be identified, not just for each story, but also for your overall branding. A company that specializes in market research for "customer experience in banking" should make sure the phrase (and others similar to it) appears in all online communications.

Social Media Optimization (SMO)

To be "seen" by blog-specific engines requires a separate social media optimization (SMO) process and an entirely different distribution mechanism. Sending a conventional press release to bloggers is often useless and sometimes counterproductive. (Bloggers have been known to snark about releases they view as beneath their dignity.) To get the word out to bloggers, it is better to set up a microblog with its own URL via a blogging site such as WordPress or Blogger. This will help your social media release get coverage by blog search engines such as Technorati, Google Blog Search, and so on. A unique site also allows bloggers to link to you.

Your social media release also needs some elements that a conventional release does not—links to video content, auto links to e-mail, print, bookmarks, shared link icons, and real simple syndication (RSS) feeds, as well as links back to microsites on your web site for more information.

Media Relations

Traditionally, public relations experts develop contacts with journalists, editors, broadcasters, and other information disseminators on behalf of their clients. When picking the media for your campaign, keep their target market in mind, as well as your own. Everyone likes to see one's name in large-circulation media like the *Wall Street Journal* or *Bloomberg Business Week*. But a trade journal or blog, such as *Bond Buyer* or marketwatch.com, can not only be a better placement, given your target market, but may also be easier to get into, especially if you get to know the key reporters, editors, and bloggers.

To cultivate the individuals who cover your market, make sure to introduce yourself at trade shows. Let them know if there are important breaking stories. Invite them to attend if you or your spokespeople are giving a speech or holding an event. Ask if you can put them on your e-mail or blog list. Getting on a media influencer's contact list as a subject-matter expert or someone to bounce ideas off can lead to a gold mine of publicity. Each time you or your spokespeople are quoted as industry experts, your company's reputation is reinforced.

Best Practices for Planning Media Campaigns

1. Determine the individual media of importance to your company and/or your target markets. For example, a company that sells services to banks might investigate such outlets as *American Banker*, *ABA Banking Journal*, and bai.org/bankingstrategies.
2. Find the appropriate contact names at these publications. This might be the reporter who covers a particular beat (for example, the banking reporter at the *Wall Street Journal*) or a blogger who specializes in ebanking. There are directories which provide this information but they are often out of date. Though time-consuming, it is preferable to contact each media source by phone or e-mail to get the right contact name and contact details.
3. Contact the individual on a one-on-one basis. With the traditional press, this is usually done by means of an e-mailed press release followed by a phone call. For a backgrounder or introduction, the PR specialist might set up a face-to-face meeting between the journalist and a company spokesperson. For a major news announcement, there might be a press conference, or a leading publication might be offered an "exclusive" opportunity to have the story appear before anyone else.
4. In addition, press releases are usually sent out "over the wires." Wire services include prnewswire.com, prweb.com, and other mass distributors. There is a cost associated with using wires to distribute your press releases, which could vary between several hundred to several thousand dollars depending on the desired distribution.

When trying to reach bloggers it is critically important, as with any media, to know what they write about and the topics they cover. Read blogs, comment on them, and become part of the blog community. Bloggers may more readily respond to pitches if you have provided feedback on posted content and provide RSS feeds.

Although radio may not reach as broad an audience, it should be considered for every consumer press campaign. It is a highly segmented medium, which means that there is probably a radio program in your local market that is targeted to your particular demographic segment. There are stations directed at every age group and ethnicity. There are thousands of talk radio shows, all looking for editorial content—that is, someone to speak intelligently about a topic of interest to listeners. Radio interviews can be recorded and added to your web site as a podcast.

Dealing with the Media

Many corporations discourage employees from speaking with the press or using social media to comment about company activities. From a corporate perspective, controlling the message assures consistency and reduces the need for "damage control" when an unauthorized spokesperson makes a mistake. There are also compliance considerations for any financial company that is regulated by a state or industry authority.

If you are in a position to interact with journalists, bloggers, or other opinion influencers, it's important to know the rules. Think of the people in the media as if they were very special clients. Remember, their days are deadline-driven, so always ask if it's a good time to talk if you call them. And remember that even if they cultivate you as a source, they don't work for you. Their job is to write fairly, not necessarily favorably. The following practices will help you to work effectively with the media:

- **Be positive.** Adversarial relationships will not go far. Reporters have stories to write and deadlines to meet—what is important to you may not be important to them. Make sure you and your spokespeople deal with every journalist objectively and honestly.
- **Know the publication and its target audience.** Take a look at the web site to read older posts or back issues. Check the editorial calendar and media kit to understand the audience and make sure your message will be relevant to the reader.
- **Know what you are going to say before you call.** Before you get on the phone, jot down your talking points. Introduce yourself and be clear and concise when pitching your story.
- **Never promise what you can't deliver.** If you commit to getting information for a reporter, make sure you provide it before his deadline. If you can't deliver, let the reporter know as soon as possible.
- **Make sure you or your spokespeople are trained in handling the media, especially for broadcast interviews, where you need to respond quickly and clearly.** Having a session or two with a professional media trainer will give you far more confidence, as well as some knowledge of how to better control the interview.

Tips for Successful Media Interviews

- Be prepared. Go into the interview with core messages, and try to cover them during the interview.
- You are the expert. Be confident.
- Support your story with facts, figures, examples, and anecdotes. They help build interest and credibility, and they give the reporter specific, useful material for his/her story.
- Use quotable, colorful language (not jargon). You may be one of several people a reporter interviews for a particular story. If your comments stand out, they are more likely to be used.
- Build "bridges." Don't just answer the reporter's question. Find ways to go beyond the answer to get to your messages—or to move away from a tough or negative question. Transitional phrases will help you accomplish this:
  - Let me put that in perspective . . .
  - Let me step back for a moment and give you some background . . .
  - What that means is . . .
  - That's an important point, because . . .
- Use "flags." Highlight your key messages by preceding them with phrases:
  - What's most important is . . .
  - The key thing is . . .
  - The three critical factors are . . .
- Avoid repeating negative language in a reporter's question. When you do, the negative words are then coming out of your mouth—and may be quoted! Without repeating the negative language, frame your response as a positive.
- Don't let reporters put words in your mouth. Be alert when questions start with phrases like:
  - Wouldn't you agree that . . .
  - What you're telling me is that . . .
- If necessary in these situations, clearly indicate your point of view with expressions like these:
  - I'd characterize it differently . . .
  - Actually, I see it very positively . . .
- Understand that with a reporter, you're always "on." Anything you say—from the chit chat at the beginning of an interview to your farewell comments at the end—is "fair game" for the reporter to use.
- Don't rely on "off the record." It's too ambiguous and uncertain, especially given the instantaneous nature of digital communications today. Assume anything you say could appear in print or online.
- If a reporter throws a barrage of questions at you, don't be overwhelmed. Pick the question that best helps you get to a message point. Let the reporter re-ask questions if you haven't answered them to his/her satisfaction.

- Don't ever feel you have to respond instantly to a reporter. Find out what the interview is about, when the deadline is, and then call back once you have prepared your messages. You can also set time limits. Typically, 20 minutes is sufficient to tell your story, while also being responsive to the reporter's questions.
- Attitude is message. Let your expertise, your enthusiasm, your passion come through in conveying the story that you—and only you—have to tell!

TV Tips

- Remember, TV interviews tend to be short (usually about three minutes) and work best when there's a back and forth "volley" between the reporter and the interviewee. Keep your responses focused and brief.
- Avoid wearing clothing that is too busy (patterns, plaids). Stick to solid tops and understated, simple jewelry.
- Sitting forward in your chair will help you appear engaged and attentive.

Provided courtesy of PR firm Cooper Katz (cooperkatz.com).

- **Follow up intelligently.** It is a good idea, after sending a press release to a traditional reporter or editor (but not a blogger), to follow up with a phone call. Editors can get an overwhelming number of press releases every day. Reminding an editor of the subject of your press release may pique her interest. She may ask you to send the release again. Do so, marking it clearly "Information requested by [name and date]." Then follow-up once more. The more relevant the information is to the audience, the more likely the press release will be used and phone calls returned.
- **Above all be ethical.** Never misinform, and be careful what you omit in the service of spinning your story. If you don't know the answer, say so, and get the answer. If you can't reveal certain information, say so.

Public Relations for Every Budget

Public relations is generally considered a relatively inexpensive marketing tool, but the costs can add up depending on what you are trying to achieve. Still, effective PR can be achieved on any budget. The list below gives some ideas, going from no budget to hundreds of thousands of dollars.

- Pitch local organizations that might be interested in having you as a speaker. If you're a financial planner or certified public accountant, for example, you will likely be welcome to talk to a wide variety of groups—from garden clubs to church groups to local parent/teacher organizations and local civic associations. If your service is more specific, find an organization that fits your target market.

- Contact local or trade publications or web sites to pitch a signed article or white paper. For example, a CPA might offer to write about business deductions that are often overlooked. Unlike a press release, or even a press interview, an article with a byline allows the writer to maintain control of the content, and underscores your positioning as an expert in the topic.
- Contact local radio station news and community-service programs to suggest interview topics.
- Respond to any comments about your firm or your specialty on blogs and social networks. Adding feedback and answering questions can position you as an expert for journalists researching your area of expertise.

Online Positioning as an Expert

Quicken Loans, an online mortgage provider, has been a leader in using internet tools in innovative ways. When "Yahoo! Answers" was introduced in 2007, Quicken Loans was an early participant, creating the "Home Loan Guru" profile and answering consumers' questions. Being wise to online publicity, Quicken Loans followed one simple rule: "Answer the question. Don't tell them how great Quicken Loans is. Don't tell them how they will benefit from its products. Don't tell them anything except what they ask."

Yahoo! picked Quicken Loans as one of its first "Knowledge Partners" in the "Answers Real Estate and Renting" category. This cemented Quicken Loans as a recommended and trusted source of information about mortgages, real estate, and finance. Feedback has been almost entirely positive. Though not conceived as a revenue generator, the Yahoo! positioning has paid off in increased site visits and closed loans directly attributable to the promotion.

Source: http://www.womma.org/casestudy/examples/content-sharing/how-quicken-loans-became-a-yah/

- Attend targeted trade shows and conferences, even if you can't afford to have a booth. Talk to vendors about their business needs. Meet with organizers and officials to discuss the criteria for conducting a seminar or participating as a panelist at upcoming events.
- Create a special event in conjunction with a nonprofit partner. For example, a bank branch might sponsor a local church picnic or a Girl Scout camping trip. Make sure the local press knows about it. (See related sponsorship and event information in Chapter 6.)
- Hire a PR agency to spread the good word about you and your firm. A retainer arrangement can run from a few thousand dollars for a small agency doing routine press releases to $25,000 a month or more for a large PR firm that performs numerous tasks beyond basic publicity, including development of communications strategies and media training for top executives. Shorter-term services—two to six months—often can be engaged à la carte for a specific campaign or announcement. A good PR firm buys you much more than its ability to write and distribute press releases. In most instances, a well-regarded firm can open doors to reporters and editors, as well as "centers of influence."

Handling Bad Press

When you or your company receives bad press, your first inclination may be to fight back. Usually, that's a mistake. If the charges are true, the best course is to publicly acknowledge the problem and fix it. Although confirming bad news—even if it's not your fault—can hurt your reputation in the short run, the pain will pass quickly, and you can move on. In the long run, your reputation will probably be strengthened by your quick action. Of course, if there is any risk of legal liability, you should consult your attorneys before making any statements.

Financial services firms have not always been willing to admit their mistakes or to publicly offer corrective action. The bad press surrounding securitized mortgages was not helped by denials, hanging tough, and failure to punish the guilty. A firm that took a strong stand and said, "we've made a mistake, and we are correcting the problem, and here's how we're doing it," would be in a far better position.

Although crisis management is outside the scope of this discussion, Table 5.2 gives a brief overview of possible responses. In the event of an actual crisis, be sure to consult a professional.

TABLE 5.2 Responses to a Crisis

Situation	Strategy	Advantages	Disadvantages
Misinformation being spread about your company	Go on the offensive with the accusers or the media for spreading rumors	Gives stakeholders rebuttal points; gets your story out	May fan the flames and cause the media to look for other potential wrongdoing
Information is true but not presented fairly	Defend your position by making spokespeople available, being open to the press	Gives your company the opportunity to set the facts straight and improve employee morale	Spokespeople may appear defensive
Your company cannot respond for legal or other reasons	Avoid press as much as possible; apologize and explain reasons for avoidance	Reduces potential legal liability	Makes company look like it's hiding something
Your company is at fault	Engage the media; hold a press conference announcing changes to address the problem; use the Internet to reach stakeholders	Gets the story out and over	Only works if you really fix the problem

Source: Adapted from Irv Schenkler and Tony Herrling, *Guide to Media Relations*, Prentice Hall Series in Advanced Business Communications, Upper Saddle River, NJ: Prentice Hall, 2003.

Measurement

There is no simple way to measure the return on investment (ROI) of PR. Traditionally, PR success has been measured in impressions, mentions, and coverage. Today every PR distribution wire service provides online statistics and listings of pickups, although in most cases this simply means that the press release has appeared on a particular publication's web site.

When Any PR Is Bad PR

Mega-insurance company American International Group (AIG) became the ugly face of the financial crisis of 2008. Not only was the company criticized for causing the meltdown, but some of its managers were personally threatened by angry consumers.

In order to defuse some of the anger, AIG hired several public relations firms to, in its words, "counter misleading statements about the company." Far from calming the crisis, AIG's hiring of PR counsel only fanned the flames. CNBC's Rachel Maddow was among several commentators who criticized the company for spending public money to fix their public image. The outcry was so great that Congress even called for hearings on the waste of government resources.

The moral: sometimes PR can hurt more than it helps.

A more accurate determination of whether a particular campaign has met goals is to conduct a survey before and after the campaign to determine lift in whatever is being measured—recognition, positive attitude, buying intentions, and so on.

One important measure of PR success is an improvement in search-engine rankings for key words. These metrics should be checked frequently as they not only show the success of your efforts, but will also frequently translate into bottom line improvements in revenues.

Note

1. "How Journalists Use Search & Social Media," http://www.toprankblog.com/2010/02/journalists-search-social-media/

CHAPTER 6

Sponsorship and Event Marketing

Sponsorships build credibility for the company, demonstrate corporate caring and good citizenship, communicate the brand's philosophy to the public, and build employee morale by involving employees with their communities.

The last time you attended a sporting event, concert, art exhibit, or local public event, how receptive were you to the products and services being promoted? Following the event did you go online to learn more or mention the sponsor to a colleague? Sponsorship of events and causes is a subset of public relations. It is used primarily as a brand-building strategy, although it has other benefits, such as building customer loyalty and motivating employees. Unlike, say, trade show or seminar marketing (discussed in Chapter 10), its primary goals are not usually immediate leads or sales.

There are tens of thousands of sponsorship properties chasing businesses that are looking to have their names associated with an event, cause, or organization. If golf is your game, there are opportunities at the local, regional, and national level that range from less than $1,000 for a local golf outing sponsorship to $10 million or more if your company chooses to be the title sponsor of a prestigious PGA event or NASCAR season. If your company is a supporter of the arts, there are museum exhibits, concerts, and hundreds of worthwhile organizations that support artists of all types. If you prefer educational initiatives, there is not a high school or college in the country that wouldn't name a scholarship after your company, as long as you fund it. Not all sponsorships cost a lot of money. A community bank or independent financial adviser might sponsor a local Little League team for less than $500. In exchange, the company's name is emblazoned on each team member's uniform.

There is no lack of opportunity. The challenge is finding the event or sponsorship—whether local or national—that best meets your objectives.

What Is the Value of Sponsorships?

Sponsorships are a way to cut through ad clutter. A survey found that 45 percent of respondents noticed the companies and products that sponsor events; 42 percent believed that the companies and products that sponsor events are of high quality, and 28 percent claimed they would buy from the companies that sponsor these events.[1] NASCAR is particularly known for its devoted fans. Depending on the product and driver, as many as 94 percent of fans purchase the product of the NASCAR sponsor over any other product in the category. They are also more likely to have positive feelings about NASCAR sponsors than about non-sponsors of competing products.

Among the benefits of sports or cause sponsorship:

- Build brand awareness by associating a company's product with an organization of importance to its target market. Brand awareness is further extended through advertising, public relations, social media, and other efforts that surround the sponsorship.
- Shorten the sales cycle. Getting the company's name known through sponsorships helps purchasers relate the company's products to a cause or team that customers also support. Many buyers would rather purchase a product with which they have an affinity.
- Maintain and strengthen existing relationships. Sponsored events provide opportunities to entertain clients in ways not typically available to the general public. Client-only receptions, celebrity "meet and greets," and event packages including tickets and parties can be created for clients and key prospects.
- Demonstrate to attendees a company's expertise through seminars and exhibits in conjunction with the sponsorship.
- Improve employee morale by providing employees with tickets to a sponsored event, encouraging volunteer activities with a sponsor organization, or holding internal contests for sponsorship-related prizes.

Locally, sponsorships help to identify and link a company to the community it is serving. Sponsorships build credibility, demonstrate a sense of corporate caring and giving, communicate the brand's philosophy to the general public, and most important, get employees and management out into the community among clients and prospects.

Insurers Get in the Game

Property/casualty insurance offers little room for differentiation and most customers choose an insurer solely on cost.

One way insurers have found to resist being a commodity is to attach their name to a popular sport or team. In recent years, Allstate has added partnerships with Major League Soccer (MLS) and U.S. Soccer. Farmers paid $600 million for naming rights to Farmers Field, a sports and events stadium in downtown Los Angeles. Esurance has become the official car insurance of college football's PAC-10 Conference. These deals reflect the growing importance of sponsorships as a platform to gain a point of differentiation.

Source: "Sponsorship Remains Fertile Ground for Property/Casualty Insurers" IEG, February 22, 2011. www .sponsorship.com.

What's the Value of a Blimp?

With two pilots and a crew of twelve, the MetLife blimp costs more than $6 million a year to operate. As a brand icon, the value of the blimp more than pays for itself many times over, when it appears at local events and on national television for major sporting events. Because the blimp provides aerial shots of the event to the networks, it doesn't pay product placement fees, thereby getting free exposure worth millions of dollars. MetLife has extended the brand value of its popular attraction online through the blimp's own web site (including a request form to have the blimp fly over your event), a Facebook page, YouTube videos, and a Twitter feed.

As competition among financial services companies grows for share of clients' wallets and attention, companies have become less differentiated. Financial companies, in particular, are looking for new and versatile ways to sell relationships, not just products.

Sponsorships give companies the opportunity to communicate with their audiences in personal and direct ways. Visa, for example, leverages its NFL sponsorship arrangement to provide exclusive experiences for Visa clients, including a Visa and NFL co-branded online portal to one-of-a-kind NFL experiences. MetLife, which has sponsored an award for human resources excellence, targets human resources professionals, to whom it sells employee-benefits programs.

Cause Marketing

Tying into sponsorship of a charitable event or creating a program in support of a charitable cause can greatly increase brand value. One study showed that 86 percent of global consumers believe that business needs to place at least equal weight on society's interests as on the business' interests.[2]

American Express (AmEx) virtually invented cause marketing with its 1983 sponsorship of the refurbishing of the Statue of Liberty. By pledging to contribute a portion of each dollar spent on the card, American Express greatly increased card usage. AmEx saw that linking its name to a good cause offered multiple benefits. For example, since 1993, AmEx has supported Share Our Strength, an anti-hunger program. Originally, AmEx was looking for a way to mollify restaurateurs who were complaining about the costs of accepting the AmEx card. Contributing part of every dollar spent on a meal in a restaurant not only raised millions for the charity, but served numerous marketing ends, including increased usage of the AmEx card and increased business for participating restaurants; improved image in the community of both the restaurants and AmEx; measurably improved cardmember satisfaction; and enhanced pride of employees working for American Express.

Choosing a Cause

Many companies donate based on the causes dear to the hearts of senior management. A more strategic way of combining marketing with charitable giving is to identify causes that are valued by your market segments or that support strategic goals.

Financial institutions looking to get a lift from younger customers sometimes choose earth-centered organizations to support, as these are popular among younger consumers and are non-controversial (see examples in Chapter 8, Social Media Marketing).

Beyond finding causes that are dear to customers and support your brand, some other issues to consider:

- Is the organization sound? When you pick a cause to support, you hope that the relationship will last over time. A one-shot is not as valuable as a continuing partnership: Do your due diligence to make sure your cause will last.
- Check out the track record of the charity on ranking web sites such as http://www.bbb.org/us/charity/ and also investigate its financials. If possible, run a search on key

---

Let Your Clients Choose Your Cause

Chase got publicity mileage and considerable goodwill for using social media to direct its corporate giving. The bank designed a promotion to give away $5 million to organizations chosen by its customers. It invited its Facebook fans to nominate non-profits, then vote to determine which organizations received Chase's philanthropy funds. The top 100 organizations getting the most votes received $25,000 each, with additional $100,000 contributions in subsequent faceoffs. Chase essentially harnessed the networking muscle of non-profit organizations and their devoted followers to help publicize its charitable campaign.

National Bank Supports Local Causes

One of Bank of America's (BofA) successful sponsorships has been its 15-year old "Museums on Us" program, which enables Bank of America and Merrill Lynch cardholders to visit popular cultural landmarks, free of charge, on the first weekend of every month. Participating organizations include national and regional art museums, science and history museums, zoos, aquariums, and gardens in communities across the United States.

As a national bank, BofA is often viewed as a monolith in competition with local banks and credit unions. By supporting local organizations, BofA makes itself more neighborly, generating a halo effect from its support of local groups.

---

personnel and board members. Nothing can deflate your brand faster than launching a campaign with an organization that has image problems.

- Learn as much as you can about the organization's donors. There should be significant overlap between the charity's target markets and your own. One private bank found that there was a sizable Asian donor base for a chamber music group and partnered on special events aimed at that community.
- Make sure the charity has the ability to pair up with your business. The sponsored organization will be carrying much of the load for your joint efforts. Evaluate the organization's public communications—print ads, web site, Twitter feed, and Facebook pages—to assess their fit with your marketing culture. Ask about their experience in cause marketing and partnering with for-profit companies.
- Actively involve the sponsored organization in your efforts. They know their cause better than you and can give you valuable information about how best to incorporate it into a campaign.
- Involve your employees. Find out what causes are important to them and make sure to get them engaged and motivated once you've picked a cause. Some companies offer their employees paid "volunteer" time, allowing them to work with the company's partnered non-profit.

For a cause-marketing program to be successful, it must be planned and executed as a partnership. Both the for-profit and non-profit partners must have a stake and mutually agree on milestones, deliverables, and measurements.

Activating a Sponsorship Program

Along with the direct donation, sponsorship carries additional costs for ancillary activities, events, and programs developed to leverage a sponsorship. Typically, a company will budget anywhere from $0.50 to $1.50 for each sponsorship dollar spent, in order to "activate" their programs.

Activation programs include many elements:

Contests. Both online and off-line offerings can range from free tickets to auto-
graphs and "meet and greets" at local events to all-expense paid trips to attend
events at faraway locations.

Giveaways (premiums). These are items such as balls, caps, and other products
with the sponsor's logo. These items can range in price from a few cents to
whatever your budget will bear.

Corporate entertainment. Luxury boxes or premium seats at sporting events and
concerts fall under this category. This perk should be reserved not only for
your best clients and prospects, but for those who are ready to buy.

Advertising and public relations. Successful sponsorships are synergistic. Getting
the word out about the sponsorship improves the return on sponsorship dollars while generating positive image building for your organization.

Client communications. These can take the form of email, statement stuffers,
newsletters, Tweets, Facebook postings, and so on. The communications can
be targeted (for instance, sent only to customers who will be able to take part
in the event), or they can be disseminated to the entire client base, particularly when the sponsorship supports a charitable cause. Letting clients know
about such activities builds goodwill

Making the Most of Your Sponsorship

Sponsorship planning should take a three-phase approach that includes pre-planning,
onsite activities, and post program follow-up.

Prior to the Start of Sponsorship

Building internal support for a sponsorship is a key element for success.
Garnering the necessary support should begin only after you are satisfied that
the event fits strategically with the company's objectives and a clear set of
metrics has been identified to measure the event's success.

Insider Access

Sponsorships can provide an extraordinary experience—something the client will
remember for a lifetime. Sponsor a team, and you can bring clients onto the field just
before the start of the game or into the locker room. Sponsor an exhibit, and guests can
see it before it opens to the public. Guests can sit in the best seats during a concert and
perhaps meet the musicians backstage. A New York Stock Exchange specialist firm has
invited clients to equestrian events featuring horses owned and trained by one of its
senior executives. Going to the winners' circle is an event not easily replicated.

- Communicate the proposed sponsorship to your various constituencies—senior management, the sales force, key marketing teams, corporate communications department, and any other area that will be directly impacted by the sponsorship.
- Build a team of cross-functional experts to assist in the planning, implementation, marketing, and internal and external communication of the sponsorship. If internal resources are not sufficient, there are outside companies that can be hired to help with event planning.
- Establish ongoing update meetings where information and ideas can be shared with everyone involved.
- Establish an activation budget, and make it everyone's responsibility to stay within it.
- Create internal excitement for the event. Develop programs that allow employees and the sales force an opportunity to participate.
- Client-facing planning should also begin long before any sponsorship events begin.
- Determine what marketing opportunities will support the sponsorship. Ask what the organizer will be doing to market the program and promote the sponsors and how you can leverage these marketing efforts.
- Determine where and how the company name will be displayed. What signage is provided by the organizers? Where will the company's logo appear in marketing material?
- Determine if speaking opportunities are available. If so, meet with organizers early in the planning to discuss potential opportunities.
- Communicate the company's involvement to your target audience through email, social media, letters, flyers, invitations, and targeted advertising.
- Determine if opportunities exist to create "mini-events" for key clients and prospects that will add value to the sponsorship.
- For a sponsored event, invite key clients, prospects, or community leaders. Schedule time to meet with them during the event.

During a Sponsored Event

- Be visible. Make sure the company is well represented at the event. If appropriate, provide company attendees with shirts or hats that can be easily spotted in a crowd or on television.
- Be prepared. Have extra tickets or event passes available for your best clients or key influencers.
- If appropriate, set up a hospitality area for employees, clients, prospects, and other guests. A hospitality area makes a great meeting location and gives invited guests a rendezvous point.
- Have a photographer on hand. Pictures make a great keepsake for guests and can be used in both personal follow-up and more broadly distributed communications such as newsletters.

Following a Sponsored Event

- Send thank-you notes and pictures to guests.
- Follow-up on business-related conversations that took place during the event.
- Meet with the sponsored organization to debrief what went right and wrong. Determine what can be corrected before agreeing to participate again.

Measuring the Effectiveness of Sponsorship

When planning a sponsorship, you should set both short- and long-term objectives for awareness building, increasing market share, and increasing retention and referrals. Also, set criteria for evaluating how the event will help achieve desired marketing objectives. The formula for measuring the success of a sponsorship will depend largely on its goals.

> **Building awareness and brand value.** Measurements will be similar to those you use for advertising and public relations: Pre- and post-sponsorship surveys can help quantify increases in awareness and positive attitudes toward the brand. Measure press coverage, hits on the sponsorship's web site, number of Facebook friends, and other relevant data points. Equivalent value can be measured by estimating the value of the sponsorship in terms of equivalent costs of advertising, public relations, and other brand-building tactics.

Measuring Return on Sponsorship (ROS)

More than ever, measuring results is becoming mandatory. A survey conducted by the ANA (Association of National Advertisers) (ANA) and IEG found that nearly 80 percent of marketers recognize the need to measure sponsorships in order to justify expenditures to senior management and to demonstrate results to the internal groups that fund the activity.

Bank of America had even more pressing reasons to measure return on its sponsorship dollars. Criticized for spending taxpayer bailout money on an expensive sponsorship of the NFL, BofA defended its actions in a public statement:

"Our relationship with the NFL is a carefully managed and heavily evaluated business that generates profits for our shareholders that are many multiples of what we pay the NFL." Bank of America revealed that for every dollar the bank spends on sports sponsorships, it earns back $10 in revenue and $3 worth of net income.

Bank of America also noted that it takes any prospective deal to a panel of bankers to evaluate its potential to drive revenue in different lines of business before committing to the sponsorship.

Sportsbusinessdaily.com, February 23, 2009

Relationship building. Compare relevant data on retention, upsell, and referrals before and after the sponsorship. A private bank determined return on investment (ROI) by using a control group: It measured increased sales and referrals for customers in Asia who were exposed to a sponsorship to those in other geographic regions who were not.

New sales. If the sponsorship includes direct sales opportunities, track data points such as number of sales leads, conversions, and new revenue. Tracking and measuring outcomes not only lets you know whether your event was successful but also enables you to make necessary changes to enhance future results.

The keys to successful sponsorships are careful research, cooperative planning, and measurement.

Some ROI measurements are easier than others. If an investment bank that buys naming rights to a stadium wins the business of financing that stadium, ROI is clear. But if an insurance agent sells a policy to a client at a golf tournament, is it fair to credit all of that revenue to the sponsorship? What about the cost of the sales executive's six months of cultivating the lead? And what if the sale comes six months after the event—how is the revenue allocated?

Not all sponsorships can be quantified by ROI. Another measure sometimes used is Return on Objective (ROO). While ROI measures the impact of a sponsorship on the bottom line, ROO offers qualitative metrics, such as employee goodwill or product satisfaction. Companies interested in brand building put a premium on data like media exposure and surveys measuring awareness and perception. Each sponsorship should set ROO benchmarks and measure against them.

Notes

1. "Cause Marketing's Power Shown in MediaLab Study," Causemarketingforum.com (http://www.causemarketing forum.com), September 1, 2003.
2. Edelman 2010 GoodPurpose study, http://www.edelman.com/insights/special/GoodPurpose 2010globalPPT_WEBversion.pdf

CHAPTER 7

Interactive Marketing

Many of the tactics described in this book focus on one-way communication from the marketer to the prospect. Advertising, PR, sponsorship, and event marketing—whether online or offline—are all essentially one-way communications.

Interactive marketing is two-way communication, whether through direct mail or through electronic or cellular media. A web site is a one-way (sometimes called broadcast) tactic. While there may be interactive elements to a web site ("contact us," online chat, etc.), it is primarily a means of providing information to the end-user without necessarily seeking the end-user's response. A direct campaign, on the other hand, is actively seeking interaction with prospects, customers, or influencers.

Personal selling, some aspects of trade shows, and all other one-to-one selling techniques are interactive. This chapter looks at a number of techniques that a marketer can use to drive a personal response, from e-mail to snail mail to mobile marketing to smartphone apps. Social media is discussed in Chapter 8.

Interactive marketing is not new. The classic way of finding new customers for insurance and brokerage accounts has long been cold calling. It is a method detested by most callers and recipients. But for those without a book of business, it was regarded by sales managers as the way for newcomers to start. (With the advent of "do not call" lists in the early 2000s, telemarketing to individuals who are not customers has become much more uncommon.) Banks have long used direct methods of getting new customers, such as handing out premiums such as pens and water bottles, to bring new customers into the door. Credit card companies have long been major users of direct mail.

Techniques and Goals of Direct Methods

Direct methods work differently than broadcast advertising. Considering the AIDA model (awareness, interest, desire, and action), the primary aims of broadcast advertising are awareness, interest, and desire. Direct methods, on the other hand, are meant to stimulate the action component, whether that is to sell products or services to new customers, generate leads for sales force or other follow-up, or drive traffic to a web site or branch.

Targeting for Tax Season

One of the advantages of interactive marketing is that it can be customized and highly targeted. H&R Block switched from generic messages to ones tailored to distinctive life-cycle segments. Targets included new movers, new parents, new homeowners, and newlyweds.

One version of a mail piece targeting recent movers read, "New digs. New deductions!" with copy expanding on the message. The names and addresses of nearby H&R Block locations were included with the message. These targeted messages were substantially more successful than the earlier, broad-based campaign.

Source: "H&R Block Ramps Up DR in $100 Million Campaign," *Direct*, March 15, 2002.

It's not just the goals that distinguish direct marketing from broadcast advertising. It's also the ability to measure whether the goals are achieved. There is rarely any swift and sure method to determine how successful broadcast tactics are at reaching their goals. With direct methods, you will often know how successful a campaign is within hours or days. Not only does this enable you to find out quickly whether a given promotion will achieve its goals, but it also permits you to test and make changes "on the fly" to bolster results.

Personalization

In addition to different goals, direct marketing employs different methods of persuasion than do broadcast methods. One key difference is that direct methods can be personalized. Personalization can be as basic as using the prospect's name in the salutation or as complex as greeting an online customer with a listing of recent purchases and suggestions for new purchases. The most important component of personalization is choosing the right offer for the right targets. Making sure that the offer is going to the right people (or conversely, making sure that the people you are planning to reach are getting the right offer) will spell the difference between success and failure.

E-mail Marketing Considerations

Sending e-mail to someone who has not asked to be e-mailed is spam and should be avoided. While there are reputable brokers who sell third-party e-mail lists, including lists of those who have signed up to be on these lists (known as permission-based or opt-in lists), response rates are generally very low (less than .001%). This type of unasked for e-mail only makes sense for marketers who are sending millions of e-mails—and there is that spam problem again.

On the other hand, e-mailing to people who have asked to receive your e-mails—whether they are customers or individuals who have signed up to receive your e-mails (referred to as a "house list")—is extremely effective. According to the Direct Marketing Association, e-mail to house lists brings in $43 for every $1 invested.[1]

Improving Opt-In Rates

Retailers (such as amazon.com) can get high opt-in rates by offering discounts and coupons. Financial services firms generally don't have the type of "product" that lends itself to these devices. On the other hand, financial marketers have a lot of content that could be of interest—everything from web site interactive tools ("how much will you need to retire?") to white papers. The higher the perceived value of these offers, the more people will opt in. Content driven, social media marketing is discussed in Chapter 8.

When seeking opt-ins for a house list, certain best practices will improve your success rate:

- *Make opt-in easy.* Many financial marketers ask too many questions before they will allow someone to download a white paper or subscribe to a newsletter. The key is getting the interested party to sign up—you can ask for other information later. Just get their e-mail address to start. Building a relationship takes time—view the first opt-in as part of a process, not an end in itself.
- *Offer user control.* Always ask for preferences on how often email opt-ins wish to be contacted, preferred format (e.g., text only or HTML, mobile, etc.), and preferred content if you have multiple e-mail offerings.
- *Acknowledge the opt-in.* If someone downloads your white paper or subscribes to your newsletter, send a welcome message. Better yet, send something of value—a different white paper, a link to preferred content—to thank them for signing up.

Goals of E-mail Marketing

Once you've developed a house list, what do you do with it? Some use e-mail to stay top of mind—a salesperson might send a monthly e-mail to let customers and prospects know about a new product feature or to pass along an interesting link or article.

Unlike retailers, few financial organizations use e-mail to generate outright sales. Some exceptions: If a prospect has investigated a product online (by, for example, using a tool to generate a quote for car insurance), a follow-up e-mail can lead to a sale. E-mail is also very effective for cross-selling and up-selling current clients (see Chapter 11 on Relationship Marketing). Business-to-business (B2B) marketers will often use house lists of prospects as lead-generators for the sales force, who generally follow up by phone.

One highly effective use of e-mail marketing is as a referral source. It is very easy to forward an e-mail and most people do forward items of interest to others. A salesperson might routinely send clients newsletters, white papers, or press clippings

FIGURE 7.1   Influences on Purchase Decisions

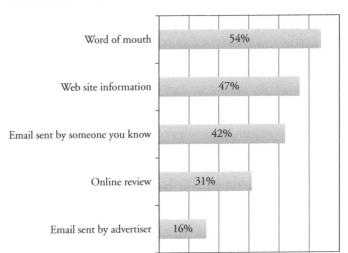

Source: "Annual Interactive Marketing Survey, *Chief Marketer,* "April 1, 2011. http://chiefmarketer.com/mobile/interactive-marketing-survey-overview-0401bq4/index.html

of interest. Asking the client to pass it along to another interested friend or colleague is an easy way to get noticed. In the consumer arena, sending a link to an interesting video or web site can help start a viral chain. Not only do you get more people interested in your message, but the recipients are also more likely to trust or buy from you. A survey by Experian found that 42 percent of purchasing decisions were based on an e-mail received from someone the buyer knew personally (see Figure 7.1).

Improving Response Rates

One of the key benefits of direct marketing (including e-mail and direct mail) is the ability to measure the impact on response of every variable in a direct package, from the size of an envelope to the subject line of an e-mail.

Because there are so many variables that can affect response, there is no simple answer to the question, "what is a typical response rate?" In fact, there is no single definition of what is meant by "response rate." But because direct results can be measured, there are certain rules of thumb to improve the response rate—however it is measured.

> **The list.** For direct mail, the list used is a key component of response rate. (A rule of thumb is 40-40-20: response is driven 40 percent by the list, 40 percent by the offer, and 20 percent by the creative). As with e-mail lists, customer lists will always perform better than prospect lists. For rented lists, there can be a huge variation in response to the same mailing to different lists. The services of a good list broker are critical.

What is a Response?

For direct mail, response is relatively straightforward—you either hear from the prospect or you don't. (There are, as always, complications. A letter may lead someone to go into a branch or make a call, where the response is not traced back to the original mailing, for example.) For e-mail, there are several metrics that can be monitored. Among them:

- **Open rate.** What percentage of the recipients opened the e-mail.
- **Click-through.** What percentage clicked on a link in the e-mail.
- **End action** such as downloading a white paper, requesting more information, texting to a phone number, making a purchase, and so on—whatever it is the marketer has set as the campaign goal. This is similar to a direct mail response, because it asks the recipient to actively respond and often, to identify himself for further marketing follow-up.
- **Return on investment (ROI).** This is the key metric and not always easy to determine. It would seem a simple matter to measure the sales generated through the current promotion divided by its cost. But for many direct marketing efforts, full value is not realized until well after the promotion ends. Credit card issuers, for example, may not realize profitability on any one mailing for years. They have developed metrics to enable them to estimate what percentage of new cardholders will remain, for how long, and how much profit they'll bring. Using this estimate of lifetime value enables the issuers to include future returns in their profitability analyses.

Other ways of measuring return on a promotion include the value of referrals to the sales force. Keeping the sales channel filled with quality new leads is an important aspect of many financial service promotions on both the consumer and institutional side. Although it may take months or even years to convert a lead into a sale, the profitability analysis of the campaign needs to account for expected future sales. Figure 7.2 shows some metrics commonly used by marketers for e-mail performance.

FIGURE 7.2 Metrics Used to Measure Interactive Marketing Performance

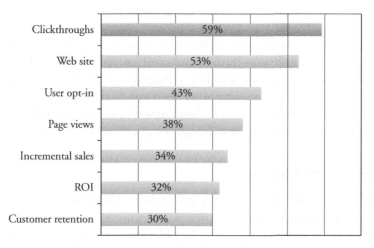

Source: Adapted from Experian Marketing Services, "The 2011 Digital Marketer: Benchmark and Trend Report," April 4, 2011, www.emarketer.com.

The offer. The nature of the product, its cost, and its uniqueness will impact response. A credit card offer will draw more than one for life insurance. Offering a premium—a free Starbucks gift card or a contest—will draw more response than the same offer without the premium. Whether it leads to more qualified responses is questionable. Experience has shown that a premium should be related to the product being sold in order to draw qualified leads.

The creative. The variables here are numerous. Not just the copy and art, but seemingly minor distinctions—such as whether to use a real stamp or a meter, or the length of a subject heading—can impact response. A split test may be worthwhile if the size of the mailing is sufficient to make results meaningful.

Integrated marketing. Other marketing efforts that run alongside your mail campaign will lift response. In B2B, a pre-phone call to ensure delivery information and a follow-up call after will lift response by a significant amount.

Multiple mailings. The number of mailings will improve response up to a certain point. Studies have shown that it can take two to five mailings or e-mails to get a satisfactory response. One investment company raised the number of re-mailings to those who had responded to an offer for a free portfolio analysis from two mailings to five. Doing so raised the number of converted sales from 30 to 66 percent. However, there is diminishing return on mailings beyond this point and too many e-mails may lead a prospect to opt out.

Teasers and subject lines. The teaser on the outside envelope of a mailer and the subject line of an e-mail are the prime real estate for getting your mail opened. The line must be appealing enough to get the prospect to open it—most "junk" mail is thrown away unread as is most e-mail. If the recipient won't recognize the "sent by" name, make sure the subject line explains what the communication is about. However, most browsers will only display about 30 to 40 characters, so you've got to make your description brief. Avoid looking like spam (or being filtered as spam) by avoiding such words as "free" or "money." Avoid all caps, exclamation points, and other spam-like devices.

Timing. Both postal mail and electronic messages will do better if timing considerations are considered. A private bank sent engraved invitations for a seminar to its high net worth clients in Brazil in February, forgetting that this is prime summer holiday season in the Southern Hemisphere. In the United States, people tend to be off work in July to August and December, so they may not receive messages sent to their office addresses. E-mail messages sent overnight will often be deleted because of the volume of spam first thing in the morning, while the same messages may be opened if received later in the day.

Electronic Factors Affecting Response

Many e-mail servers only show text messages, omitting images unless the user requests them. Gifs and jpgs will not be displayed, so make sure important information is in the text.

Make sure the response link is "above the fold." Many people will glance at an e-mail but won't bother to scroll down. Putting the link near the top will improve response.

Permission to e-mail does not permit the marketer to use text (SMS) messaging. You will need a separate opt in to use this form of communication.

Different devices display differently. Viewing e-mail is different on different browsers and mobile devices. Test the e-mails on a variety of devices to make sure they display correctly.

Your e-mail provider should advise you about specific parameters for sending to various e-mail servers and to help keep your lists clean and up to date.

Social Media Premium for E-mail Marketing Campaign

AmEx has used Facebook to deliver customer value and create an online community. For its related e-mail campaign, AmEx cleverly came up with a way to turn Facebook "likes" into measurable cardholder activity.

In its "Link, Like, Love" campaign, AmEx sent e-mails with the subject line: "Amex turns your "likes" into things you'll love." (Depending on the browser, this might end up as "Amex turns your "likes" into things you'll . . .") The offer asked the cardholder to link her Facebook account to her AmEx card. From within Facebook, AmEx provides "special deals and experiences we've selected for you based on your likes and interests, as well as the likes and interests of your Facebook friends." When the customer clicks on a deal, it is automatically charged to her AmEx card.

While the e-mail is personalized, it is not customized. A stronger promotion would use AmEx's database of information about the customer to give examples of what the user might like and the associated deals. Nevertheless, the promotion is a good example of using e-mail to promote cross-channel relationship building and up-sell.

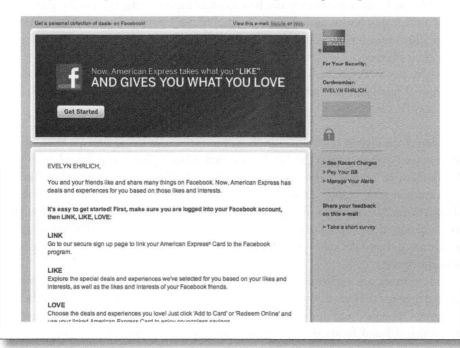

Mobile Marketing

In addition to e-mail and text (SMS) messages, mobile phones—especially smart phones—offer opportunities to marketers that are just beginning to emerge. Since consumers are using their phones to check balances, make account transfers, and other financial transactions, it is a relatively simple matter to trigger auto messages reminding them of additional products and services that fit their needs. Alerts let them know when their balance is low or a payment is due.

Cell phones give marketers the opportunity to converge messaging with Point of Sale (POS)—for example, if a consumer's credit card is declined, the opportunity to offer additional credit on the spot. Bank of America (BofA) has a service that texts debit cardholders if their card is declined because of insufficient funds. The customer receives the message while he or she is still standing at the checkout counter. If the customer agrees to pay a $35 overdraft fee, BofA will allow the transaction to go through. Or customers are given the option to transfer funds or deposit more money into their accounts by 8 p.m. of the day the transaction is made to avoid the fee.

The most innovative—and most potentially profitable—mobile marketing tactics are those that use the device's built-in capabilities, such as location mapping, cameras (for scanning), or downloadable apps.

Some examples include:

- Using location sensors, MasterCard offers a free downloadable app that lets users know the closest branch of any bank.
- USAA and Chase were among the first to enable users to use their cell phone cameras to scan in checks, and deposit them over the Internet. PayPal offers a service that allows transfers from one person's PayPal account to another, simply by touching their phones.
- Putnam has a "PriceCheck&Save" app, which allows users to scan the barcode of potential purchases and see how much their money could grow if they invested it in their IRA instead.

One of the biggest markets for mobile apps is the sales force, who are huge smartphone users. For example, Fidelity has created a smartphone app for advisors that allows them to access clients' account balances, holdings and transaction history, and view real-time market news and quotes on the fly. Genworth Financial Wealth Management has created a library of advisor tools and marketing information that can be managed and downloaded from a smartphone or tablet. No more carrying literature around on sales calls—it's all inside the device and can be displayed for clients from the device.

Some firms are experimenting with Quick Response (QR) codes in advertising and signage that send responders to more information online or to a video. For example, OppenheimerFunds used QR codes to promote the portfolio managers of its municipal bond funds in adviser-targeted magazines. Oppenheimer updated the

---

Leveraging QR Codes

QR codes work best in conjunction with a special offer not available elsewhere or to deliver unique and valuable content to a smartphone. Blogger Jim Marous offers these suggestions for how they might be used:

- Supplement billboard, print, ATM, or branch marketing with video content that more fully describes a promotion or provides a special offer.
- As a supplement for a traditional product brochure rack in a branch allowing for product offers and continuously updated product information.
- Videos of staff experts talking about financial topics.
- Updated rates, competitive grids, linkage to online financial management tools, and more.

Source: Bank Marketing Strategy blog, http://jimmarous.blogspot.com/2011/04/qr-codes-are-mobile-gateway-for-bank.html#more

---

videos linked to the codes so that advisers could hear current commentary from the firm's portfolio managers.[2] TD Bank has used QR codes on bus shelter advertising to promote the locations of its branches.

Taking the idea one step further, OBEE Credit Union in Oregon developed a scavenger hunt using Microsoft's version of the QR code. Participants visited local businesses and scanned the QR tag displayed. It showed a video offering information about the merchant and took participants to the next location. Those who collected all 30 tags (by photographing them) were invited to a party and entered to win prizes including $10,000 in cash. The promotion was mostly funded by participating businesses, which paid a small entry fee in exchange for foot traffic and the video spot about their business.[3]

Direct marketing is among the most effective tactics available to the marketer. While social media generates more buzz in marketing circles, messages that are not intermediated by the entire Internet allow marketers to talk directly to clients and prospects with greater control over the message. They permit marketers to more accurately measure response. And they often result directly in increased revenue.

Notes

1. Cited in Lorrie Thomas, *The McGraw-Hill 36-Hour Course: Online Marketing*, 2010, page 175.
2. *Investment News*, December 19, 2010, www.investmentnews.com/apps/pbcs.dll/article?AID=/20101219/REG/312169999
3. "Credit Union Toys with Microsoft Tag Tech in $15,000 Scavenger Hunt," www.thefinancialbrand.com, January 14, 2011.

CHAPTER 8

Social Media Marketing

Interactive marketing is two-way communication between marketer and end user; social media marketing is multi-directional, with communications among end users as well as with the marketer. Many financial services companies have been reluctant to use social media because of this lack of control over the content of the communication. In a 2009 analysis conducted by Altimeter Group and Wetpaint, showing the degree of usage of social media by industry, the financial services industry was at the bottom (see Figure 8.1).

There are numerous reasons why financial marketers have been slow to adopt social media tools. There are, however, compelling reasons why they need to do so:

- Raise your visibility on natural search engines (sometimes called search engine marketing [SEM]). The more content you post and the more links to and from your site to other appropriate sites, the higher your position on certain key words.
- Give prospects a way to find you. Most prospects—whether consumers or institutional—do online research when they approach a buying decision. If they are interested in managed futures and come across your blog that offers regular commentary on that market, your firm may be added to their list of potential resources.

FIGURE 8.1 Social Media Engagement by Industry

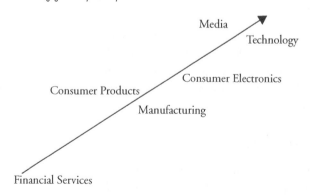

Adapted from Engagement DB Report, 2009. See www.scribd.com/doc/17666696/Engagement-Rankings-Of-The-Worlds-Most-Valuable-Brands

- Public relations opportunities—developing an online reputation as an expert in a subject area can lead to press interviews, invitations to speak at conferences, guest posts on other blogs, and so on.
- Leverage content across the Internet. Blogs can be easily repurposed as posts on Twitter; topic areas within social media sites (such as LinkedIn) can provide newsletter content; print, video, and other content can be communicated in community forums, sharing sites, and so forth.

Social Media Concerns

Financial marketers generally give several reasons why they have been slow to adapt social media:

- Loss of control
- Regulatory complexity
- Cost versus revenue
- Lack of expertise and resources

Loss of Control

Traditionally, a key part of the marketer's job was controlling the message in order to maintain brand consistency through all the marketing channels. But avoiding the social media will not prevent others from talking about you. As a rule, it is better to participate in the conversation.

"Companies always thought they had control over a brand and control over the message because they weren't hearing the conversations that consumers were having. People are always talking about your brand in ways you can't control."[1]

At a minimum, every company and individual should monitor what is being said about them—tools can range from the simple (Google Alerts) to full-scale media monitoring.

Regulatory Complexity

Lightly regulated marketers, such as credit card issuers, have been far ahead of the curve in using social media. The Financial Industry Regulatory Authority (FINRA), which regulates money managers, brokerages, and advisory firms, only released its social media guidelines in 2010 and there is still a lack of clarity around some issues. Many regulated firms are dipping their toes in social media but are reluctant to test boundaries.

Cost versus Revenue Considerations

Anyone who thinks social media marketing is a low-cost tactic has never done it. The constant emergence of new technologies—and new tools to help manage these technologies—makes the social channel one of the most complex and ever-changing

Slow Start for Wirehouse Social Media Usage

In 2011, Morgan Stanley began testing a pilot program to allow its financial advisors to interact with clients and others on Twitter and LinkedIn through "pre-approved public updates and private LinkedIn emails, invitations and introductions." Previously, Morgan advisors were only able to create profiles, but not post updates or send messages.

Morgan's advisors were also allowed to send LinkedIn InMail messages, request introductions, send invitations and participate on the site. However, reps were not allowed to "recommend" other financial advisors, nor be recommended by others because of the regulatory rules around the use of testimonials.

As FINRA-regulated broker-dealers, the big wirehouses are very nervous about letting in-house advisors use social media without pre-approval. The problem, of course, is that the very essence of social media is spontaneity and timeliness.

Despite its limitations, the Morgan initiative was actually a step forward for captive advisors who are mostly forbidden to message others on social networks. Some of the smaller independent broker/dealers, like Raymond James, actually allow their advisors to conduct "truly interactive conversations in real-time, without pre-approval."

Because FINRA regards any social media or blog post to be public, there are strict rules concerning maintaining records and meeting guidelines, making social media problematic. For more information, see FINRA "Regulatory Notice 10-06: Guidance on Blogs and Social Networking Web Sites" (www.finra.org/Industry/Regulation/Notices/2010/P120760).

"Morgan First On Wall Street to Crack Social Media Code," *Registered Rep*, May 25, 2011

---

marketing tactics. What's more, the return on the investment in time, outside expertise, and other costs is very difficult to measure.

How much is a Facebook "like" worth? How much money must you invest to get a promotion to "go viral?" What is the lifetime value of a customer who comes to you because of a view on a comparative ranking site and how does it compare to one who came in through traditional marketing methods? The answers to these questions (like many in financial marketing) are not clear.

One area that has been measured is outside the scope of this chapter—using social media for resolution of customer-service issues. Some big marketers (Wells Fargo is a notable example) have a dedicated customer service Twitter staff and have realized measurable cost savings (and saved relationships) from using that channel for problem resolution.

There has been much anecdotal evidence of LinkedIn and Facebook driving sales for individual practitioners. One mortgage broker has built up more than 1200 connections with realtors and banks on LinkedIn and no longer uses any other marketing tactics to expand his business. Financial advisors have reconnected with old friends (and their friends) on Facebook, driving new business. According to one 2010 survey,

---

Return of 100 Percent Over Expectations

Credit card companies are ahead of the curve in building return-on-investment (ROI) models to show the effectiveness of their social media marketing. American Express used social media as the primary tool for building customers for ZYNC, a card aimed at Gen Y consumers.

Using social media, AmEx invited influencers to experience the card and share their experiences online. Additional tools, including television advertising, were used to drive customers to branded online sites.

In the first nine months after launch, the card exceeded AmEx's goals by 100 percent.

ANA blog, October 28, 2010

---

47 percent of financial advisors reported having identified one or more referrals (new leads/prospects) from their social media activity and 36 percent said they had acquired new customers this way.[2]

On the whole, most experts view social media as a brand and relationship builder, rather than as an acquisition tool. Adding social media to the traditional toolbox has become standard for the largest companies. For smaller institutions and individuals, justifying the cost comes down to your objectives and your target markets.

Effective Social Media Engagement

The last of the objections—lack of expertise and resources—is addressed in the remainder of this chapter. While there are many online tools and expert consultants that can help you manage your social media efforts, like everything else, social media participation must be prioritized.

The basic marketing strategies—segmentation, positioning, and identifying objectives—should drive your social media tactics as well. To be successful, marketers must leverage their own expertise to create and deliver differentiated content that can be shared with target segments across media channels.

This is a lot of work—even for so limited a topic. So if you are going to prioritize, ask which are the tactics that are most likely to show a return on investment in attention, awareness, and action? Figure 8.2 shows a range of tactics that fall under the "social media" category with the authors' opinion of the effectiveness versus difficulty of each tactic. *Effectiveness* is defined as those tactics that are likely to result in more attention for your message. *Difficulty* refers to the amount of man hours (in-house or subcontracted) required to maintain the tactic.

Sharing Knowledge Across Social Media

An insurance company introduced a new 401(k) plan that was differentiated by its fiduciary protections for plan sponsors. One of the company's goals was to establish its expertise in helping small businesses avoid regulatory violations or employee lawsuits related to the selection of investments for the plan.

The firm hired a staff attorney who was a recognized expert in ERISA (Employee Retirement Income Security Act) law for retirement plans. To generate online interest and attention, the firm considered a number of tactics. The principles apply to any content distributed through social media.

- *Key word identification.* Develop a list of key words, such as "ERISA," "investment fiduciary" "retirement plan fiduciary."
- *Online differentiation.* Make a thorough search of existing web content on the selected key words to determine your positioning as well as appropriate links to other sites' content.
- *Microsite.* Create a microsite devoted to the topic with a distinctive URL. The company created a section within the corporate web site at www.companyname/fiduciary.
- *Blog.* Your blog is where your content begins. The fiduciary site features regular posts about changes in the law, court cases impacting small business, and other content related to the attorney's specialty, with links back to the microsite, as well as to other relevant content. For compliance reasons, commenting on the site is moderated.
- *Comment.* The attorney regularly posts comments on other blogs, networking sites where target customers gather (such as small business forums), and relevant LinkedIn groups, with information and discussion of the topic. Where appropriate, he cross-links from and to the blog.
- *Video and slide share.* When the attorney makes online presentations for advisors and small business clients, they are posted on appropriate sharing sites (such as SlideShare) and on the microsite.
- *Monitored internal discussion forum.* The microsite includes a discussion board, behind a secure log-in, for advisors to ask questions and converse with the attorney.
- *Twitter.* When new information is posted on the blog, Twitter messages are sent out.
- *E-newsletter.* This is sent quarterly to small business clients and contains content first posted on the blog.

This is far from a complete list of social media marketing tools, which are constantly changing. Bear in mind that some of this information will be out of date before you read it. Where traditional marketing media evolved over decades, every day seems to bring a new "transformative" technology to social media.

The following discussion is meant to be an introduction to general principles of using online media, rather than a specific how-to. There are many online discussions of how to practice social media marketing and many specialists and online tools to help you manage it.

FIGURE 8.2   Social Media Marketing Tactics

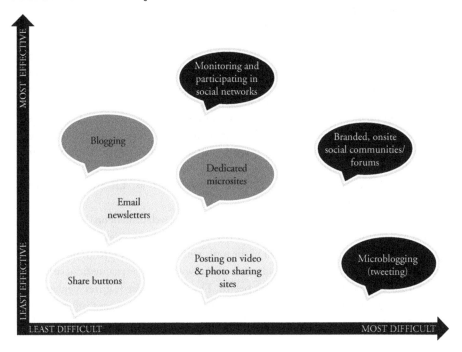

Share Buttons

It's easy to add buttons and real simple syndication (RSS) feeds to web sites, blogs, and other content . The payoff isn't large, but the potential for getting your content shared by your users is worth the small effort.

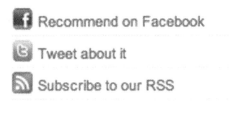

E-mail Newsletters

E-mail newsletters are discussed in Chapter 7 Interactive Marketing and Chapter 11 Relationship Marketing. The key point is to share content you create with your e-mail subscribers. You may think they will find the information on your site or your blog but that means relying on them to come to you. You will get more response, more quickly, if you go to them.

Blogging

Blogging isn't hard—you probably have lots of content lying around. Blogging well is more difficult and getting noticed is hardest of all.

Blogging has changed over the years. In the beginning, it was often used as a way to share personal content with friends and family. That application has largely migrated to Facebook and other social networking sites. Today's blogs—at least the influential ones—are about sharing knowledge and ideas.

To be an influential blogger you have to find a niche that will appeal to your target segments, that is differentiated from your competitors, and that has something unique and insightful to say about your subject matter. Successful blogging leads to having a following and being recognized as an expert in your subject matter.

Most financial companies have developed a lot of content for their own sites but fail to distribute this content beyond their own borders. This is changing. Said one money management marketer, "We no longer think that our dot.com site is the center of the universe. We need to break down the walls and provide content in lots of different places."[3]

Tips for Successful Blogging

Successful blogging takes time and effort. Some guidelines include:

- Do your homework. Keep up with your subject specialty, know what information is being published on other sites, and strive to find new content.
- The more original your content, the better. Team up with a research firm to publish results of surveys or conduct your own survey research. Create a top 10 list. Conduct interviews with opinion leaders. Have something meaningful to say that will be of value to your target audience.
- Avoid self-serving content. No one wants to read a blog that is a sales pitch.
- Establish a regular publishing schedule and keep to your deadlines. Weekly is ideal; monthly is probably more practical unless you have a lot of meaningful information to communicate.

Bad Blogging

An Australian Bank, NAB, closed down its blog "after one of its employees posted comments posing as a legitimate customer. At first, the impostor denied he was a bank employee, but forensic Internet analysis proved that all his comments originated from an NAB server inside the bank. The revelation immediately sparked a Twitter firestorm, followed by waves of protests across the blogosphere."

Thefinancialbrand.com, October 27, 2008, http://thefinancialbrand.com/2824/nabs-social-media-failure/

- Have a distinctive voice. If you're a community bank or credit union writing about your community, make it friendly and personal.
- Embed visuals. Photos of a charity event you sponsored, videos illustrating home improvements for a lender, charts and graphs for an investment blog, and so on will make your content more lively and engaging.
- Respond to comments. Some blogs will not allow comments for regulatory reasons. If you want others to comment, respond to them.
- If permitted by your regulators, respond on other sites related to your subject. Share links among non-competing blogs and LinkedIn groups. The more incoming links to your site, the higher your search engine rankings and the more people will find you.
- Be up front and honest. Posting comments on your site or other sites that purport to come from a disinterested observer will cause you grief.

Branded and Co-Branded Microsite

A good example of using a microsite around a topic is shown in Figure 8.3. This multi-media campaign is for RBC's Blue Water project, which is designed to raise awareness about water resources (and RBC Bank). In addition to its own branded microsite at bluewater.rbc.com, the bank also created a separate, co-branded site with National Geographic at www.nationalgeographic.com/bluewaterproject. These sites aggregate content from Twitter and Facebook and provide unique landing pages for visitors and incoming links. Content includes videos, games and quizzes, and a panoply of online tools. Because of its non-commercial subject matter, it has been successful in generating interest: Its Facebook page has more than 25,000 likes and its YouTube video series has been viewed more than 3,000 times.

From a branding perspective, the campaign has certainly created good will for the Canadian bank.

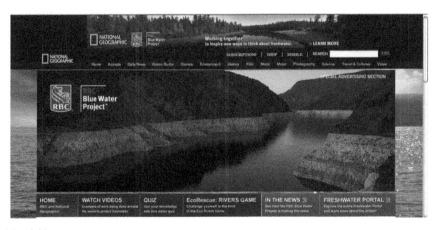

Co-branded Site

Microsites

One of the keys to social media success is having a "hub" for content that attracts visitors naturally through search engines, the blogosphere, and social networking sites. Some marketers create URLs within their web sites where activity about a particular subject is directed, but this makes it more difficult for interested readers—and web crawlers—to find. Setting up a separate microsite takes a bit more work and coordination, but it can pay big in generating traffic.

Micro-blogging/Tweeting

Micro-blogging is used for communicating short messages (less than 140 characters on Twitter) and associated links. Similar to phone text messaging and IM (instant messaging), Twitter is the best known of micro-blogging sites. Services such as Foursquare, which allow people to communicate their location, can also be considered micro-blogs. This discussion focuses on any site that permits instant communication among audiences in small bursts of text or links.

How Advisors Use Social Networks

Advisors are successfully using networks such as LinkedIn to reach new prospects, increase awareness of their practices, differentiate from other practices, and increase revenues, as shown in Figure 8.3.

FIGURE 8.3 How Advisors Use Social Networks

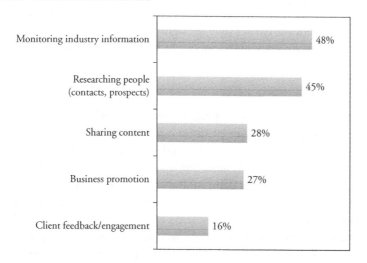

Source: Adapted from American Century survey of advisors, 2010, reported in Blog.socialware.com, September 20, 2010.

Hosted micro-blogging sites are particularly useful for collaboration within an organization, by facilitating interaction among experts in multiple locations. For example, many of the stock and options exchanges have implemented internal micro-blogging sites to give traders the ability to communicate among themselves. A profession that relies on up-to-the minute information and microsecond advantages for its livelihood has an appetite for sharing news and information as quickly as possible.

The Chicago Mercantile Exchange (CME) Futures & Options Exchange and the Chicago Board of Options Exchanges (CBOE) use Twitter to keep traders up to date. Bloomberg's IM feature can be considered a kind of Twitter for bond traders. One user says these trading-floor information exchanges are "almost as good as a trading pit on the old floor."[4] Numerous Twitter accounts are dedicated to specific industry segments—for example @CUTweetTrack for credit unions and @ CommunityBanks. Keeping up with industry gossip and news is a prime micro-blogging application.

Marketers are also using Twitter and Twitter-like micro-blogs for events. TD Ameritrade set up a Twitter site to highlight messages and to allow attendees to interact during a conference it sponsored for registered investment advisor (RIA) clients. Attendees actively tweeted about events, speakers, and content.

For marketing to consumers, Twitter and its kin have offered mixed blessings. Many organizations are successfully using Twitter to monitor and resolve customer-service issues. Employing dedicated staff to intervene before complaints go viral serves an important function for both customer retention and reputation management. But while large institutions, such as Wells Fargo, can afford to build Twitter teams, smaller financial marketers may find the cost of the effort greater than the potential benefit.

According to the blog The Financial Brand, "you'll have to determine whether there's value in engaging an audience that will likely total no more than 1 percent of your existing customer/member base. Financial institutions that provide service and resolve customer issues via Twitter may see significant value, while those hoping to use Twitter as a broadcast or marketing tool might be sorely disappointed."[5]

Online Communities

There is a fine line between microblogging and social networking, and most of the information that can be conveyed on one platform can be communicated on all of them (i.e., status updates, links, Q&A, etc.). They also tend to overlap audiences, so your Facebook fans may also be your Twitter followers. Software can help you manage incoming and outgoing postings so that they are communicated to and from all your accounts.

Online communities go beyond social networking sites, such as Facebook and Linkedin. They include any place where users talk to each other, including consumer rating sites such as yelp.com, specialized forums, and content-sharing sites such as trading sites, photo and video sharing sites, wikis, and many others. Social networks directed to financial professionals include riabiz.com, ifalife.com, and hedgehogs.net (for hedge fund professionals). There are hundreds of sites where users trade stock tips or discuss personal finance.

While participating in all these communities is overwhelming, even for the largest financial marketers, a strategic approach that focuses on your target markets and your marketing objectives should enable you to narrow your social activity to the essentials. A company in the retirement plan business, for example, might target small business communities and content sites that focus on retirement-related issues. A marketer seeking to influence RIAs would want to participate on sites such as riabiz.com, financialplanning.com, and registeredrep.com.

For those in the consumer space, it is important to limit participation to the most relevant sites and to have clear goals for each. Schwab's business to consumer (B2C) marketers, for example, identified Facebook, Twitter, and YouTube as their three key social channels, and outlined objectives and strategies for each. Schwab's Facebook objectives are to provide meaningful updates that fans can relate to and find relevant, and try to appeal to a broad audience with company news, fan feedback, financial articles, interactive polling features, and commenting capabilities. Twitter objectives include listening, engaging, and connecting with thought leaders, consumers, journalists, and media.[6]

Building a Social Networking Presence

Social media blogger Mike Langford at blog.socialware.com has identified a five-step process to help users find their way on social networks, from which the chart in Figure 8.4 is adapted.

FIGURE 8.4   Building a Social Networking Presence

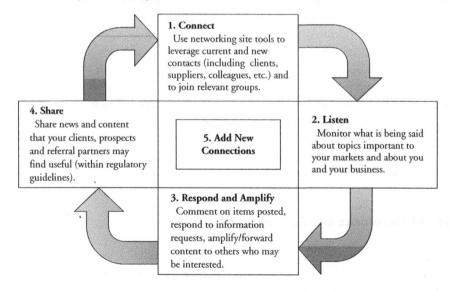

FIGURE 8.5   Negative Comments Decision Tree

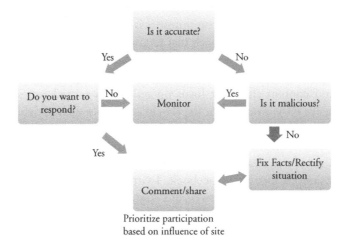

Handling Negative Comments

Negative comments can be posted on blogs, ranking sites (such as yelp.com), Twitter, Facebook, and other networking sites. You may not want to respond to all of them. The diagram in Figure 8.5 shows a decision tree of whether to respond and if so, how to respond.

When you come across a negative comment, ask first if it is accurate. If it isn't, you may not want to fan the flames by giving it credibility. It may have been posted by a disgruntled employee or a competitor and the best way to respond is to ignore it. Monitor the situation to see if the false information is getting any traction. If it is, step in.

If the negative post is accurate, see how you can fix the situation. If it concerns an individual account, reach out to the customer on the same site inviting them to speak or e-mail privately. The public invitation shows that you are concerned about the problem without compromising confidential information. If it is a more generic problem—that is, "why doesn't the branch have Sunday hours?"—you can answer publicly if you want to do so.

Not every site has equal weight—you need to prioritize to make sure you are directing your resources toward the sites most likely to benefit you. For example, a research firm that recruits mystery shoppers may be mentioned on mystery shopper sites, including complaints about slow payments. This could be a priority if the firm needs to recruit shoppers from the site. But it is unlikely that its bank clients will be concerned about this issue, so it may not be strategically important to respond to these complaints—even if they're accurate.

Social Networks as Marketing Channels

Beyond information sharing and customer service, what marketing functions are served by social media? Here are a few ways marketers have used social media for customer acquisition and retention.

Do Consumers Get Better Service via Social Networks?

SunTrust Bank monitors conversations customers have about the bank on social media, responding where necessary to handle customer service issues. "It is a savvier client who thinks that if they engage with us publicly and have this conversation in this open forum we will hear what they have to say," says a SunTrust spokesperson.

The perception that institutions will respond more quickly and more positively in an open forum is probably true. An unresolved complaint, registered by phone or e-mail, only puts one customer at risk. On Twitter or Facebook, the complaint may be read by the entire community around that person. And a complaint on a ranking site can be read by thousands of people—including some who are prospects actively seeking the exact service that customer is complaining about.

Many institutions allow customers to interact with them through their Facebook account. Since many younger customers use Facebook as their default home page, it is imperative to enable this option if this is a target segment. A survey of 3,000 online consumers in November, 2010, found 11 percent connected to their financial institutions through social channels. "The 18-to-25-year-old market clearly told us that they want to interact with us online," noted one credit union manager.

Source: blog.Socialware.com, January 15, 2011.

- Building followers with prizes

  It has become common to seed Facebook, YouTube, and other sites with contests and sweepstakes to stimulate social activity. MasterCard, for example, has leveraged its Priceless campaign to solicit photos of "priceless moments," which are judged by the crowd for prizes. Other contests include Seattle Verity Credit Union's "Verity Mom" (become a paid blogger), TD Canada's video contest for best environmental film, which carries prizes for both individual winners and the winners' colleges, and Scotia Bank's tie-in with a movie chain where participation pays off in free movie tickets.

- Crowd-sourcing

  Chase Bank has innovated in using crowd-sourcing as both a market research and acquisition tool. An early effort asked a group of college Facebook users what they were looking for in a credit card. From their responses, Chase learned that they would like to be able to pool rewards, so that a sorority or club could earn rewards for a common purchase (such as an HDTV). Chase not only gained valuable insight into its market, it also created the first card to meet this market need.

  Seeing the value in this crowd-sourced feedback, Chase did it again in conjunction with IHG (Intercontinental Hotel Group) to develop a next-generation Priority Club rewards card. In 2009, IHG and Chase collaborated with members of IHG's customer loyalty group to design a credit card that includes an annual free night good anywhere in the world and increased point earnings at

IHG hotels and for everyday purchases. The new product generated an 80 percent increase in new accounts.[7]

- Sponsorship

    Many financial institutions have co-branded their online promotions with causes, such as the environment, that resonate with a younger customer. (See sidebar on RBC's Blue Water project cited earlier in this chapter.) Co-branding gives the marketer access to social networks through both their own and their partner's fan base. It also helps generate publicity—both Chase and AmEx got back many times the cost of the donation in media coverage by sponsoring contests to promote a favorite cause. Chase's $5 million Facebook promotion ultimately led to over 2,500,000 "fans" on the bank's page.

    Even smaller financial marketers can benefit from local online communities. Communities organized around a high school football team or the local Chamber of Commerce can be tapped for a cross-promotion. (See Chapter 6 on Sponsorship and Event Marketing.)

- Hosting your own social communities

    Some financial institutions have successfully established social networks on their own web sites. AmEx pioneered its openforum.com for small business members to discuss business issues with other members. USAA has a community hub, including a discussion forum for military spouses. Because USAA has a narrowly defined target market (military families), it has been quite successful in drawing users to its site for social networking.

    An example of an in-house social network in the business-to-business (B2B) space is Nasdaq Community, Nasdaq's social media hub, which offers articles, comments, questions and answers, and other content. One Nasdaq manager said

---

Regulatory Restrictions Lead to Sales

FICO, the credit scoring service, is prevented by regulations from advising customers on how to improve credit scores. To overcome this restriction, it created a social networking site where consumers can share credit knowledge, experiences, and advice with each other.

Not only has the site given FICO an active community of supporters—it has also improved its bottom line: With 10 percent of all support calls now directed to the community, support costs have decreased by 1 percent. Thirteen percent of all online sales include viewing a community page, and visitors spend, on average, 66 percent more after joining the community.

Source: http://forrester.typepad.com/groundswell/2009/10/winners-of-the-2009-forrester-groundswell-awards.html "we were astounded at the time, energy, and passion put into answering [others' queries]. People really are leveraging the intelligence of the community."[8]

- On-site ratings to aid acquisition

USAA has added customer ratings of products and services to its web site. According to Forrester, customer reviews have led to a significant surge in sales on USAA's web site. During a nine-month period in 2009, the utilization of customer ratings and reviews drove nearly 16,000 incremental product sales.[9]

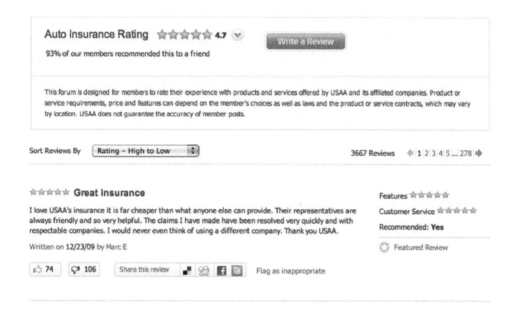

For most marketing campaigns, social media will not be a standalone solution, but will be used in conjunction with the marketing tactics discussed throughout this book. Whether social media are used to support a product's positioning or to generate incremental revenue, what is unique about social media as a marketing tactic is its ability to spiral from person to person, multiplying potential effectiveness—and potential harm. Marketers cannot "control" what is said about a product or service, but they can direct the conversation through careful strategic planning within a larger campaign. Neither a panacea nor a threat, social media are merely another tool in the marketer's toolbox.

Notes

1. "Web 3.0: The 'Social Wave' and How It Disrupts the Internet," Knowledge@Wharton, July 6, 2011.
2. http://blog.socialware.com/2010/06/28/new-survey-published-on-advisor's-use-of-social-media/

3. www.webinknow.com/2009/08/putnam-investments-breaks-ground-on-blogs-twitter-and-social-media.html
4. FOW, April 20, 2010. www.fow.com/Article/2469372/Regions/26543/Social-media-back-to-the-trading-floor.html
5. Thefinancialbrand.com, February 28, 2011, http://thefinancialbrand.com/17227/financial-followers-by-assets-customers-employees/
6. ANA blog, June 2011.
7. Forrester.typepad.com, October 28, 2010. http://forrester.typepad.com/groundswell/2010/10/winners-of-the-2010-forrester-groundswell-awards-b2c.html
8. FOW, 20 April 2010.
9. "USAA proves the value of web site ratings and reviews to financial services," March 16, 2010. http://blogs.forrester.com/brad_strothkamp/10-03-16-usaa_proves_value_web_site_ratings_and_reviews_financial_services

CHAPTER 9

Personal Selling

Traditionally, financial services have been sales driven. In most companies, marketers do not have direct access to the firm's clients. But as the financial industry has changed, the role of marketing has become more central. In the past, salespeople often felt marketers were obstacles rather than supporters. There is a dawning recognition that each party needs the other.

It is possible that financial companies have the most complex sales structures of any industry. Consider, for example, a company like Fidelity Investments. These are some of the selling relationships for its investment management/mutual fund product set:

- In-house (captive) phone sales
- In-house (captive) branch sales
- Third-party independent advisers (e.g., fee-only planners and independent brokers)
- Third-party wire house brokers (e.g., Merrill Lynch)
- Third-party diversified financial brokers (e.g., AXA)
- Third-party bank brokers (e.g., Chase)
- Third-party direct marketers (e.g., Schwab)
- In-house institutional sales reps who sell retirement plans to plan sponsors
- In-house institutional sales reps who sell retirement plans to plan providers
- Third-party pension brokers who sell retirement plans to plan sponsors
- In-house institutional sales reps who sell managed accounts to wire houses
- Brokers at these firms who offer managed accounts to their clients
- In-house sales reps who offer managed accounts directly to end customers

That's at least 13 different sales channels for just one type of product (see Figure 9.1).

The old saying is that financial products aren't bought but sold. This has certainly long been true in life insurance. For most people, buying financial services is a chore. It is not fun to shop for a mortgage, an annuity, or a retirement plan. If it weren't for a salesperson's persistence, many people would choose to avoid the whole decision-making process.

But the industry is changing in ways that have made the role of the marketer more important than before: Competition across sub-segments (overlapping insurance,

FIGURE 9.1   Major Sales Channels

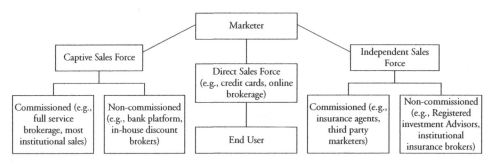

bank, and brokerage firms), industry consolidation leading to bigger competitors, and the increasing role of technology, to name a few.

There have also been significant changes in how the sales force works. Selling commissioned products, like insurance or stocks, used to be relatively straightforward. You sold a stock, you got a commission. Today, sales-force compensation emphasizes asset-gathering, not individual transactions. The goal is to keep the customer for the long term, to build a relationship. Consequently, the role of marketing has become more central. Witness the rise of the Chief Marketing Officer (CMO), a role that didn't exist within financial services until recently. Marketing can provide the tools that enable the sales rep to anticipate client needs. Analytical software can let a financial adviser know when clients are at critical points—when they are in danger of leaving, when there is an opportunity to sell them something, when they need a call to keep them satisfied.

Traditional Relationships between Sales and Marketing

The relationship between sales and marketing differs significantly among the various financial sub-segments. Some segments have no sales function. Marketers that deal directly with the end user—such as credit card issuers, some no-load mutual funds, and direct insurance sales—acquire and service their customers without the aid of a relationship-based sales force.

Some sub-segments, such as banks and credit unions, sell primarily through a noncommissioned sales force. This is an example of "top-down marketing" in which a central group—either a product group or marketing group—sets goals and then instructs its staff to fulfill the directives. For example, a bank may decide that spring is a good time to sell home equity products. The marketing department oversees an ad campaign, branch signage, perhaps creation of a customer incentive, and telemarketing, direct mail, and Internet campaigns. Each branch is given a sales goal, and contests or other means are used to "mobilize the troops." The branches with the most home equity loans originated are given a special prize, or the branch manager takes them all out for a pizza.

A BRAG Book for Branch Marketing

Although the central marketing and product functions control the overall marketing effort, individual bank branches often have some flexibility and some (limited) budget to create their own local marketing efforts. Sometimes these efforts are supported by a central marketing group. For example, Chase created a local marketing group that served as a kind of internal promotions agency, creating both customized and generic materials for the branches. The local marketing group even supplied a print (and later, online) catalog, called the BRAG book (Branch Resource Action Guide) listing the various materials available to branch sales staff. These materials included everything from ads, press releases, and by-lined articles to signage, seminar kits, direct response postcards, and many other items.

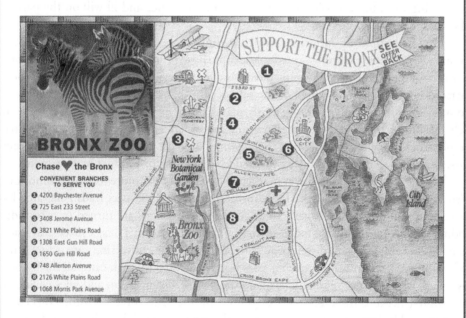

A customized local postcard campaign for Chase branches in the Bronx

Consumer banks have a mix of commissioned and noncommissioned sales personnel. The commissioned people include institutional sales executives, middle-market and small-business calling officers, insurance and investment brokers, and mortgage bankers. The platform workers (tellers, supervisors, branch managers) are not on commission, even though they are usually expected to push products. Top-down marketing is efficient—all decisions are centralized and marketing budgets can be allocated on a rational basis. Campaign effectiveness can be easily measured, promotions stay "on brand," and niche markets can easily be targeted.

Bottom-Up Marketing

Unlike branch staff, commissioned salespeople tend to think like entrepreneurs. They are only interested in a marketing program if it will translate to their bottom line. Sometimes called *bottom-up* marketing, in this arrangement marketing must sell the sales force first and then the end client. As an example, a major brokerage company wanted to consolidate and centralize client information in order to be able to handle any client inquiry seamlessly, whether the inquiry was to the broker, the customer service center, or online. In a bank this would be routine practice. But in the brokerage industry, the sales force traditionally maintained its own records for each rep's personal use. A broker considers his "book of business" his personal property, notwithstanding lawsuits that routinely take place when a broker leaves one firm for another and takes his clients with him. In this example, marketing and sales were at loggerheads. Marketing won, but not without a great deal of reluctance and ill will on the part of the sales force.

In most bottom-up industries, which include brokerages, insurance, and institutional sales, in-house commissioned salespeople have nearly exclusive access to clients. If the marketing department wants to reach a client, they must work through the salesperson. Finding a way to convince the salesperson that a particular product will lead to more sales may involve creating costly materials. Items such as sales guides (how to sell the product), PowerPoint presentations, sales letters, articles for the sales force to place in local publications under their bylines, local customizable print and Internet ads, and radio spots are routinely provided by marketing or product management.

In order to sell the sales force, marketers have to budget more for any promotion. Yet, at the same time, they have less control over results. Prospect leads generated by advertising, direct mail, telemarketing, or online campaigns are turned over to individual salespeople (or their branch managers) for conversion. Thus, a successful lead-generation campaign could well prove unprofitable if the conversion rate is low. And sales staff are notorious for ignoring sales leads generated by such campaigns. By one estimate, 80 percent of marketing expenditures on lead generation and sales collateral are wasted because these efforts are ignored by the sales force.[1] Another difficulty encountered by bottom-up marketers is overlapping responsibilities between the marketing and sales management organizations. In most firms, sales management controls commission rates, bonuses, sales contests, and all other forms of compensation. With its limited input over the most crucial sales motivator, marketing has limited impact on sales results.

Third-Party Sales

If the job of a marketer selling to a captive sales force sounds difficult, consider the plight of the marketer whose target is a third-party salesperson. Commissioned sales representatives may be independents, or work for banks, brokerage, or diversified financial firms. In insurance, for example, companies without a captive sales force may sell their policies through independent insurance brokers, who can recommend

Sales and Marketing Working Together

"The brand is central to everything the organization does," noted the director of sales development at American Express. "The challenge is to move away from the silos created over the years . . . between sales and marketing." To make sure the sales force always stayed "on message" and to help salespeople with increasingly complex sales, sales and marketing joined together to create a centralized sales intelligence center called "Sales Force Online." It gave the sales force centralized access to some 500 different marketing programs, including downloadable product literature, customizable presentations, and background information—such as product information, customer testimonials, and survey findings—that would help make a sale.

The sales organization chose a steering committee to identify and prioritize the most useful functions. This group of sales leaders then became the program's champions. Marketing benefited from better marketing intelligence, as it analyzed how the sales force used various programs. For the sales force, productivity went up significantly: Presentation preparation time was cut in half, acquisition costs declined substantially, and customers were getting more focused messages that led to higher close rates.

Source: "CMM Case Study: American Express' Sales Force Online," *Marketing News,* June 24, 2002, 12–13.

anyone's policy to their clients. Similarly, mutual funds, retirement funds, and other investment vehicles often sell through third parties.

As an example of the complexities of selling through third parties, consider the pressure on mutual fund companies to develop new means of compensating salespeople. In the past, brokers were primarily commission-based, and were paid commissions through "loads" (i.e., sales charges)—including front end, back end, and contingent loads. Today, many financial advisors work on an asset-based charge (a percent of assets under management) and do not collect commissions on sales of individual products.

Since there are more than six thousand mutual funds in the United States, getting a mutual fund (or closed-end fund or annuity or money manager/wrap account) in front of a third party has become as difficult as getting a new grocery product on a shelf. And like groceries, brokerages started charging for "shelf space." In this arrangement, fund families paid "revenue-sharing" fees to the brokerage firm in order to gain access to the brokerage's sales force. In addition, some funds used "directed brokerage" in which a fund company agreed to direct a specified amount of trades to a brokerage in exchange for greater access to its sales force.

Along with other questionable sales practices, such as compensating sales forces with 12b-1 fees and using sales contests to raise commissions for brokers who sold certain funds, these actions drew the scrutiny of regulators. And while some of these practices have been reformed, fund marketers still face the problem of breaking through the clutter to sell to third-party brokers.

When the Sales Force Won't Sell a Product

Getting the attention of sales agents is not an easy task. A major insurance company exited the retirement plan business in the late 1990s because it could not get enough brokers—captive or independent—to sell the product. Why? Most of the salespeople at the insurance company's own agencies did not have the necessary licensing to sell investment products—and were not sufficiently motivated to commit the time, money, and effort needed to get licensed. On the other hand, independent retirement plan specialists, who were licensed to sell annuities, already had relationships with a small group of retirement plan providers and saw no reason to expand the list. Even though the insurance company offered higher commission rates, agents were not interested in learning a new product line, dealing with underwriters who might balk at their clients, or putting their reputation on the line for a company they weren't sure was going to stay in the business.

High-Net-Worth Sales

The high-net-worth (HNW) market is served by many types of financial firms, from trust departments, private banks, and upscale investment banking firms to individual financial advisers or "wealth managers." Although $500,000 in investable assets will get someone HNW status with some financial advisers and firms, it may take $5 million or more to qualify for a private banker. For Goldman Sachs to handle a portfolio, the cost of entry will be $25 million or more.

One of the most competitive areas is the managed-account business, in which money managers compete to handle the accounts of individuals through their brokers or bankers. The money-management company must first be selected by the institution to participate in its managed-account program and then must be picked from the list of approved managers by the individual adviser for his or her client. Not only is there intense competition among money managers, but the number of banking and brokerage firms that offer managed accounts has skyrocketed in recent years as they have become popular with HNW clients.

Institutional Sales

People who become commissioned sales reps tend to be independent, which makes them difficult for marketers to influence. As one goes up the selling ladder to those who deal with the really big-ticket sales, particularly to institutions, the role of marketing becomes less and less important. These are sales that require a painstaking, one-on-one process, often involving long intervals between initial contact and closing the sale.

Consumer sales cycles can take hours (for e-mail campaigns), days, or perhaps weeks. Institutional sales cycles—getting a new client for securities trading, investment banking, institutional asset management, plan consulting, credit analysis, risk

Selling to the Corner Office

Brokers who sell separately managed accounts (SMAs) tend to be those with the biggest books of business—the ones whose success has put them in the corner office. In fact, just 5 percent of the adviser force at most wire houses and regional broker-dealers generates 80 to 90 percent of managed-account business. To reach these superstars, a smaller money manager created a targeted campaign. Its "Influential Advisors" were invited to an intense, three-day training program featuring a roster of well-known portfolio managers, wealth management specialists, and featured speakers—and of course, high-end entertainment.

The CMO, who started her career with a brokerage firm, understood that what brokers need most is support. The money manager's sales reps sat down with heads of brokerage sales areas and found out what kinds of programs brokers find most useful. They provided modeling and profiling tools, seminars, programs to which brokers could invite their own clients, customizable newsletters, presentations, white papers, and other tools to help brokers keep abreast of new ideas and build their practices. "It's not enough to give the salespeople interesting information," the CMO noted. "It has to be actionable." As an example, she cited a survey the firm conducted on entrepreneurial wealth. Rather than simply presenting the survey results, the company put together a sales kit that walked brokers through the information and showed them how to use it to interact with their own clients and prospects. These were expensive programs, but they paid off for the money manager. According to the CMO, the return in new business was as much as one thousand times the amount spent.

management, prime brokerage, back-office services, or technology—routinely takes years. There are several reasons why this is true. First, the number of people involved in making a decision is usually high, which means going back over the same ground again and again. Second, some of these products are only purchased by a given customer once in a blue moon: For example, a company only seeks an underwriter for an initial public offering or a specialist firm for its stock listing when it is going public. Third, it is very difficult for outsiders to reach the decision makers. They are hidden behind support staff and subordinates. Last, many of these business decisions have traditionally been made for personal reasons. Selection of an investment banker, trading broker, or trustee is still likely to be based on which club the buyer and seller belong to or having been fraternity brothers in college.

At the highest levels, the people who make the sales do not think of themselves as salespeople, but as partners, underwriters, or bankers. They don't market—they network. A marketing expense might be flying a potential buyer in one's private plane to Scotland for a round of golf. But even below this rarefied level, systematic market planning and plan execution is not much practiced. Instead, most institutional sales take place opportunistically. A salesperson whose commission-based income can exceed that of the firm's CEO will call clients regularly, looking for cross-selling opportunities

---

Consumer Tactics for Institutional Sales

Traditionally, the institutional sales force has been supported with marketing tactics such as booths at trade shows, sponsorship of specialized road shows or product exhibitions, and other events for clients (golf and tennis tournaments or training seminars held at lush resorts). The purpose of these events is to give the salesperson the opportunity to get to know the client and build a relationship—or put another way, to "schmooze" the client in order to build long-term good will and to cross-sell.

The treasury services department of a major bank has found success by modifying tactics traditionally associated with consumer marketing. For example, when the treasury services area entered a new geographic marketplace, the sales representative for the region compiled a list of his top prospects and asked the marketing department for help in getting through to the chief financial officers of these large corporations. Marketing came up with an appropriate premium—a silver key chain whose hang-tag was a Mercator map with the company's logo—and created a custom box, letter, and brochure. The salesperson sent a few of these items out each week, by messenger, to serve as an icebreaker. As a result, he was successful in securing appointments with most of his prospects. Two months later, the marketing staff followed up with a reception for these new contacts at a prestigious private club that featured other areas of the bank, thus leveraging the earlier promotion into a companywide sales success.

---

or referrals to potential new clients. Or she may expand her network by serving on boards of nonprofit or trade organizations, joining special-interest groups involved in industry issues (lobbying Washington, for example), and attending high-level industry conferences. This relationship building may be supplemented with seminar and trade show selling, event sponsorship, and other "marketing" tactics, but for the most part, institutional sales are passive rather than active. Most institutional salespeople disdain retail-type tactics such as direct marketing. Although this attitude is changing and institutional sellers are beginning to think more strategically, most wholesale institutions have a long way to go before they are true marketers.

Changes in the Sales Distribution Model

The holy grail in marketing today is relationship building. Almost all companies—not just financial firms—have shifted their emphasis from one-time transactions to ongoing relationships. Financial firms whose sales representatives possess personal, one-on-one relationships with the client have a built-in advantage when it comes to relationship building. And yet, many organizations that have the good fortune to have strong ties between their customers and their sales reps are trying to nudge the salesperson out of the picture. Many brokerage firms, for example, are "migrating" clients with lower assets to online and phone channels.

It is understandable that brokerage firms are seeking to change the relationship between client and broker-adviser. For one thing, there's the matter of profitability— each full-service client can cost the firm more than some smaller clients provide in profits. Second, the cost of brokers at the call center is much lower, both in commissions and in overhead. More crucial for the firm, the goal is to redirect the relationship from client-broker to client-firm. The broker model has always presented a problem for firms with commissioned sales forces. If the broker decides to leave, in most cases the client will go along.

To counter this, companies have put complex systems in place to initiate communication with clients as soon as a salesperson resigns. Firms know they have very little time in which to retain the client. To many clients, the salesperson *is* the company. If clients are happy with the advice being received, they will follow the adviser. The reality is that there is no way to prevent clients from moving their accounts to other firms if they so choose.

This perception that the broker "owns" the client makes brokers hard to manage. Firms that attempt to cut compensation rates may see a massive outflow of their top salespeople, who can always find another brokerage that will give them a bonus for making the move with their book of business. These individuals can also become independent and collect 70 to 90 percent payouts on sales compared with the 25 to 45 percent they typically get at a major Wall Street firm.

In a situation such as a change of ownership, this exodus can have major repercussions. For example, sales of products by Prudential Securities brokers declined an estimated $50 million in the first five months of 2003, following the sale of its brokerage division to Wachovia (now part of Wells Fargo). Wachovia lost nearly 15 percent of Prudential brokers, who jumped to rival firms following the acquisition.[2]

As a result of all these factors, brokerages and other commission-driven firms are looking for ways to move clients to a new relationship with the institution, not the broker. Even high-value clients are encouraged to use all available transaction channels, including online and phone, as well as transacting through their broker. Brokers are getting new tools that enable them to work with clients over the Internet on an instant messaging model. While these tools are designed to improve broker productivity, they also loosen the bonds between brokers and their clients. The more tied-in the client is to a given company's systems, the less likely the client is to follow a broker to another firm.

Ironically, while commission-based companies are trying to wean customers off personal relationships with brokers, commercial banks are heading the other way. Chase, for example, instituted a personal "relationship manager" to service its small-business customers who combine personal and business balances. Why? Because small-business owners often have significant personal assets that can be captured by building a relationship based on business banking.

Advisers who keep their client relationships strong are likely to benefit their firms as well. When UBS initiated a major ad campaign announcing its brokerage's name change from UBS PaineWebber, its financial advisers were required to contact each client to explain the change. The result was few client defections and more asset inflow. (For more on relationship marketing, see Chapter 11.)

Marketing Support Across the Sales Cycle

Sales people generally view the marketing department as a source of leads and customer-facing programs, such as seminars. Salespeople believe they do the "heavy lifting" that turns a cold lead into a signed client.

But there are many ways the marketing function can and does more to support sales across the sales cycle.

- Pre-Meeting Research: An insurance company created a custom database that allows retirement advisors to scope out a company's plan in detail before arranging a first meeting. Combining both public information from 5,500 filings and proprietary data on the company itself, it can give the advisor information to guide a conversation. For example, if the plan is top-heavy (many senior people and few rank-and-file employees), the system signals the advisor to suggest a more suitable plan type.

  For big-ticket sales, marketing can provide helpful pre-meeting research based on online searches. Searches on Twitter, LinkedIn, Facebook, and other sites can help the sales person identify common interests, acquaintances, and background to build common ground to make the first meeting more productive.
- Lead nurturing: Big-ticket sales often have long sales cycles. It is critical that the sales force maintain regular contact with prospects over this period. A content-marketing program gives the sales force information of value to send to prospects on a regular basis and reminds them to do so. Valuable content includes industry reports, best practices, blog or LinkedIn posts, and other materials not directly product related but rather of interest to the specific target market (Content marketing is discussed further in Chapter 8.
- Onboarding: Once a client has been signed, they should receive regularly scheduled follow-ups, including a welcome package, courtesy calls as to satisfaction with the product/service, and additional structured communications over the first 12 to 18 months. These efforts can help turn new customers into promoters and referral sources. (For more on onboarding, see Chapter 11, Relationship Marketing.)

How Sales Can Help Marketing Help Sales

The relationship between sales and marketing is a little bit like the relationship between teenagers and their parents. Parents (marketers) try to guide the teens (sales force) in the right direction, and prevent them from making mistakes. Teens resent parents telling them what to do and insist on making their own decisions. But also like teens, the sales force may be too focused on the present and not always have the best interests of the organization in mind for the long term. For example, marketers complain when their in-house salespeople create their own client materials rather than use the materials so expensively crafted by the marketing department. Salespeople

Bull versus Opossum

Many years ago, before Merrill Lynch had a marketing department to support its institutional products, a floor trader decided he wanted his own marketing brochure. Since the trader handled mortgage options, he thought it would be clever to brand them as "options to purchase or sell specified mortgage-backed securities," or OPOSSMS, and had a design firm come up with a cute little opossum logo. When the brochure was printed and distributed to clients and the press, there was a fair amount of buzz about the "new" product. Everyone was happy until the head of retail marketing called the perpetrators on the carpet. "Merrill Lynch is associated with noble beasts," she thundered, "bulls and tigers [a product of the time]—not road kill." She was right. OPOSSMS violated many years and dollars of brand-building effort, and even though the buzz served the product, it threatened to diminish the brand as a whole.

claim they know better what will appeal to their clients. What they fail to understand is that the marketer is looking to preserve the brand image of the firm.

Sales-created promotions can trigger a number of potential problems:

- Legal and compliance errors
- Poor impression on the part of the client if there are typos, misspellings, grammar mistakes, or an amateurish writing style
- Failure to conform to brand image—the presentation of a consistent look and feel across the enterprise

Like parents, marketers can be good or bad. Good marketers support the sales force with essential information and client materials, including prospecting tools, lead-generation campaigns, help with developing successful sales techniques, product training, generic promotional material (brochures, ads, newsletters), customized material (proposals, sales letters, client reports), and trade show and seminar marketing. In return, good salespeople give feedback to marketing, letting them know what works and what doesn't, what they need, and how marketing can best support them.

Many traditional sales organizations have begun asking the sales force to think more like marketers. For practical demonstrations of how sales people can use marketing techniques and tactics, see the Appendix Applying Marketing Principles to Sales Practice.

Notes

1. Research by the Aberdeen Group, cited in Carol Krol, "Why can't marketing and sales get along?" *BtoB*, www.btob.com, April 14, 2003.
2. Imogen Rose-Smith, "Pru Tallies Cost of Talent Exodus," *Wall Street Letter*, June 11, 2003.

CHAPTER 10

Trade Shows and Seminars

Trade shows and seminars provide face-to-face contact with prospects who otherwise might be difficult to reach. They are usually qualified and are receptive to learning about products and services. As a function of their attendance at the event, these individuals have mentally and psychologically opted-in to an environment in which they are open to learning about products and services.

Sales tools like seminars and trade shows require planning: Choosing appropriate target market segments, approaching these segments in a consistent and professional manner, and searching out opportunities competitors may have missed. Whether you exhibit at a trade show or host a seminar, a number of steps are necessary to help insure success. Commonalities in planning and execution exist between the two kinds of events, but each has unique elements that must be considered and planned for.

Trade Shows

The largest challenge most trade show exhibitors face is getting attendees to visit their exhibit space. When there are often hundreds of exhibitors competing for the attendees' attention, a combination of planning, creativity, and thoughtful targeting is needed to bring the crowds to your space. Here are some crucial considerations for preparation, activation, and follow-up to a trade show:

- Assess the value of exhibiting. If you can't identify the benefit, there probably isn't any. Don't exhibit just because a competitor chooses to; it's far more important that you exhibit where your potential customers are.
- Accordingly, select the trade show based on where your target markets will be. Thousands of local, regional, and national trade shows take place each year. Consider only those that reach your target audience(s). For example, banks and mortgage lenders can often be found at home improvement and garden shows, because most attendees own homes and may be looking to use the equity to make improvements. Institutional sales executives choose shows that draw their particular industry focus. For example, prime-brokerage-services providers often exhibit at conferences for hedge fund managers.

- Investigate whether a show's size, anticipated attendees, other exhibitors, and past success meet your objectives. Contact the show's organizers to obtain a show kit, which will provide important information about exhibitors, statistics about past attendees and show hours, set-up and take-down dates and times, shipping information, and other important details.
- Budget comprehensively. Know what the total costs will be. The price of the typical 10' x 10' trade show space is just the first in a long list of expenses. In addition to the fee for the space, plan on paying additional charges for electrical power, internet service, chairs, carpeting, display lighting, wastepaper baskets, display racks, decorative accessories, set-up and take-down, shipping, materials, and give-away items. Other expenses include travel, hotel, and meals for staff who will be staffing the booth, the cost of any receptions you host, and other client entertainment. These additional expenses add up quickly and may be considerably more than the exhibition's costs.
- Organize all of the elements of the show in advance. Develop a schedule and assign people to work the booth. Share all of the show information with them. To determine staffing needs, determine the number of expected attendees and number of hours the exhibit is open. This information should be available from the show's management. Assuming contact with one-fifth of the passers-by for three to five minutes each, you can assess staffing needs as follows for a show with five thousand attendees that runs for three days: 20 percent of five thousand equals one thousand attendees who will visit your booth. One thousand attendees times three minutes per visit equals fifty hours of visits. Fifty hours divided by the twenty-one hours the exhibit is open equals two or three staff members. Based on personal past experience or information from show management, adjust the formula accordingly.
- Brainstorm ways to attract attendees to the exhibit booth. Unique or popular raffle prizes such as gift certificates to popular restaurants, or high-tech gadgetry work well. Some exhibitors use food to draw people—the smell of popcorn popping or coffee brewing can be a powerful attraction. Another idea is to create a mobile app with a searchable list of area bars and restaurants that attendees can download at your booth.
- Most shows have a social media component such as Twitter, LinkedIn, or Facebook pages. Make comments and actively participate both before and during the show. Have special offers, such as demonstrations, noted guest speakers, giveaways, and so on available during the show and publicize them on these media.
- Determine whether to display printed literature at the booth. For consumer shows, plan for 15 to 20 percent of attendees to take relevant literature. For institutional shows, it is better to send the information after the show, since most attendees will throw it away. Or consider using QR codes on booth signage that links to product information, white papers, and so on.
- Order give-away items at least six weeks in advance, particularly if they are custom-made or display a company logo. Compared with printed brochures, premiums have a much higher "take" rate. When ordering premiums, assume that 60 to 70 percent of attendees will take at least one of whatever is being offered. It may be advisable to "tier" premiums. Good prospects, who have been qualified by booth

staff, may get higher-value items than passers-by. The cost of premiums should be related to the value of the potential business. For an international treasury conference, a crystal item with an engraved logo, worth $30 or more, might be appropriate for "A" prospects. For a consumer show, a key chain or pen costing less than $0.50 would make more sense.

Breaking through Booth Clutter

Getting the attention of trade show attendees is always challenging. To help differentiate your exhibit and drive traffic to your booth, conducting pre-exhibit promotions will increase your odds of being noticed. It will take time, effort, and some expense, but it is generally worth the investment. One way to increase traffic is to let attendees know your company is exhibiting. Some shows will provide complimentary or deeply discounted tickets to exhibitors. For consumer shows, send key customers and prospects a show invitation with a pair of tickets three weeks prior to the show. For institutional shows, e-mail or call likely attendees to let them know you will be exhibiting. Invite recipients to stop by the exhibit and receive a gift. Use the show to network with current customers as well as to meet new prospects.

Another way to reach potential buyers is through an onsite seminar or event. Rent a meeting or conference room and provide refreshments. Publicize the event on the show's Twitter or LinkedIn pages, by invitation, and at the booth. Be sure those who attend your event swipe their show information so you have it for follow-up. A private event gives show attendees and exhibitors (who may be some of your best prospects) a break from the noise and the crowds of the exhibit hall. If the show itself includes a conference, another tactic is to sponsor a coffee break, lunch, or cocktail reception. Doing so will put you on the program as a sponsor and may entitle you to other promotional benefits.

The appearance of the exhibit booth is a direct reflection on the company. Although size may not matter, appearance does. Always maintain an inviting and professional space. Companies spend huge amounts to create a professional atmosphere within their booth space and don't wish attendees to see an exhibitor slouched in a chair or eating lunch. Booth staffers will not win new business by extending a greasy hand to a prospect.

Following Up Leads

Getting solid sales leads from a trade show or even getting an attendee to stop by an exhibit booth is hard work and takes careful thought and planning. Since lead generation is usually the reason companies dedicate resources to exhibiting, the number-one priority following the show must be to follow up on the leads that were obtained.

Know what needs to be tracked. Decide in advance what information you want to capture beyond name and contact information. For consumer shows without swipe cards, use a raffle to have visitors fill out their contact information on a tablet or Smartphone in the booth. You may want to ask for additional information and

Trade Show Errors

Knowing the most common pitfalls can make the trade show more cost-effective, create a better experience, and generate more of those all-important leads. When planning for the next trade show, keep the following "don'ts" in mind:

- Don't assume you know the composition of attendees and exhibitors based on the show's name. Be sure the show organizer provides attendee demographics and lists of current and previous exhibitors.
- Don't underestimate the need and value of assigning measurable show goals to each staff member, such as number of contacts per hour, number of leads per day, and number of show-related sales.
- Don't underestimate staffing needs at the booth. Staffers who are overworked, tired, and hungry can't be effective. Plan for exhibit booth staff to take a 30- to 60-minute break every two to three hours.
- Don't send staff who have insufficient product knowledge. Make sure all staff are well versed in the company's products and services. It may mean holding a training or refresher class prior to the trade show.
- Don't forget to review the list of exhibitors for prospects. Take time to "walk the show" and visit with other exhibitors.
- Don't establish physical barriers between yourself and attendees. Avoid placing tables, counters, or chairs across the front of the exhibit space. Doing so restricts access to the exhibit and places a barrier between the exhibitor and prospect. Even small spaces should be made inviting to potential prospects.
- Don't distribute expensive literature. Half or more of the literature distributed at a trade show almost immediately finds its way into the trash.
- Don't allow staff to eat or make personal phone calls while in the booth. They should look interested and available to speak with attendees at all times.
- Don't let staff close the exhibit earlier then the published show times and dates. There is a tendency to wind down early at the end of a long day and to begin packing up hours before the official close on the final day. Research has shown that many attendees use the end of the show to revisit exhibitors they are interested in doing business with.
- Don't let sales leads go stale. Follow-up within the first 48 hours is key to success.

permission to add the name to your e-mail list. Under do-not-call rules, it is legitimate to call prospects who have spoken to a staff member and requested information. If you are collecting phone numbers from a raffle form, on the other hand, you will need to get legal clarification about following up by phone. The same gray area exists about e-mail. If it was not specifically requested, it could be regarded as spam under the "CAN-SPAM" law.

Many business shows provide attendees with swipe cards containing all relevant information. Or you may collect business cards. Try to supplement these with other useful tracking data, such as size of company and product interest, for lead follow-ups. To minimize lapse time, a letter should be prepared prior to the show and then personalized and sent to every lead within 48 hours of the show's close. The letter should thank prospects for visiting the exhibit booth and inform them to expect a phone call following up on their interest in the company's product or service. Also send thank-you notes to clients who stopped by the exhibit booth. If a seminar was held, a similar letter should be sent to those attendees, thanking them for attending and alerting them to expect a follow-up phone call.

Measuring Results

Implement the following checklist to insure lead follow-up and accurate reporting:

- Make sure all attendee data, including business card information, has been entered in your database.
- Assign leads and make salespeople accountable. Determine prior to the event the number of leads an individual salesperson can reasonably respond to. Have salespeople ready to handle the excess leads or those leads in which an individual salesperson's particular expertise or territory makes it a logical hand-off.
- Assign one or more lead coordinators. A lead coordinator manages the flow of leads to the sales force, the follow-up, and the input of information into the database.
- Track appointments scheduled, appointments completed, referrals, sales by product type, dollar amounts of the sales, and whatever other information is relevant to your measurements.
- After the leads have been pursued by the sales force, you can arrive at an approximate return on investment (ROI) by dividing new business generated from exhibit visitors by the expense of the show. Be sure to include any new sales to your own invited clients. If new sales outweigh the expense of the event, the event can be considered successful. Some companies may look for a two-to-one return to consider an event a success, whereas others may look for a larger or smaller multiplier.

Seminars

In many ways, coordinating seminars is similar to preparing for trade shows. The big difference is that the roles of organizer, sponsor, marketer, operations director, and salesperson all belong to the host. From the selection of the topic, attendee mailing list, and venue selection to filling the seats and planning follow-up activities, all of the steps need to be carefully coordinated. Seminars can be highly successful or dismal failures. Although no one can control all of the factors that will attract prospective customers, there are ways to improve the odds of success.

Planning

Identify the target markets and their needs (for example, retirement planning or regulatory changes), and select the seminar topic that is important to them. In planning the presentation, determine if partners or additional experts are needed to speak on complicated or multifaceted topics. For example, a financial planner might invite an estate lawyer to participate in a seminar on estate planning.

Seminars for institutional clients are sometimes expensive, several-day affairs at top-tier resorts. Product experts and analysts, along with well-known outside speakers, conduct sessions, followed by golf or wine tastings. High-net-worth clients also require special handling. A leading private client insurer held a successful event for directors of family offices at a private, terraced suite in an upscale hotel. Clients sipped cocktails and gazed at the view of the Metropolitan Museum and Central Park while listening to speakers talk about art collecting—and insuring collections.

The larger the event and the more speakers and guests, the longer and more complex the planning process. Outside speakers should be invited at least three to four months before the event in order to ensure firm commitments. If you're planning a panel presentation, the ideal number of panelists is three. But invite four—or have a backup speaker—in case one of them must cancel at the last minute. Ideally, your speakers will confer with the organizer and one another at least a month before the event to make sure the material covered is relevant. Make it clear that speakers are there to educate the audience—not give a sales presentation. It is polite to give your speakers a token gift usually worth less than $100. Obviously, you do not need to give a gift if you are paying for a speaker's services.

Once the topic is established, the next step is to select a date for the seminar. In choosing a date and time, keep in mind:

- Are other high-profile events planned for the date being considered? This could adversely affect attendance.
- Typically July and August are not good months for seminars because of summer vacation plans, although some practitioners disagree and focus on these summer months because schedules tend to be less hectic.
- Avoid mid-December to early January because of the crush of holiday obligations.
- Avoid Sundays, Mondays, and major holidays. Some feel Friday nights can be effective if a reception is built into the evening.
- Select a time and venue that will be convenient for the target audience. Breakfast or immediately after the workday are generally good times to reach working people. Saturday mornings may be best for couples. Consider providing on-site babysitting services for couples with young children.

When selecting a venue, try to be creative. Look for locations that are unique, such as museums, art galleries, or new restaurants. This gives invitees another reason to attend. For special client events, "insider" access to behind the scenes (of a theater, sports arena, restaurant, or any venue difficult to get into) will encourage attendance.

Choose a Cosponsor

A Chicago branch of a major financial services company sent out five thousand seminar invitations to a targeted subscriber list of a well-known national magazine. The seminar was co-branded with the name of the publication in order to draw additional attention. There were 200 positive responses to the invitation, and 110 of those showed up—a respectable 2 percent response rate.

Marketing the Seminar

There is always a worry that "confirmed" attendees will fail to show up. There are several ways to improve the odds of filling the seats:

- Invitations must be sent out early enough (from two months to three weeks in advance). Make sure the invitation specifies where and how to RSVP—by phone, e-mail, or reply card.
- Phone follow-up within a week of mailing is optimal, but not always possible under do-not-call rules, unless you have a prior relationship. Consider, instead, inviting clients (whom you may call) and ask them to bring a friend.
- Reconfirm with those who have said they will be attending. This should be done two to three days prior to the seminar and should serve as a reminder and to let guests know that you look forward to seeing them at the seminar.

Even with this approach, plan on at least 25 percent of "confirmed" attendees not showing up. If it rains or snows on the day of the event, attendance will drop even more.

Response to your invitation will vary, depending on the topic, speaker, venue, list quality, and whether the invitees are customers or prospects. For a purchased prospect list and a run-of-the-mill topic, estimate a 1 to 2 percent response. This means that you will have to send five thousand pieces to fill a 50-seat room. If you are mailing to your own customers, or have a big-name speaker, you could draw 10 percent or more. If you get lucky and are oversubscribed, you can always set up a second session.

The Magic Word "Complimentary"

A local office of a financial services company held a financial-planning workshop that was advertised in the local paper. The number of attendees—zero! Why? The ad did not specifically say that the seminar was complimentary. "Complimentary" is one of the most important words to use when inviting people to a seminar, whether through advertising or invitation.

If the seminar will be marketed through newspaper or radio advertising, be sure to include a call to action—a phone number or Web address for reservations. This will provide a gauge as to the number of attendees that can be expected. Because these individuals are responding to a nameless and faceless ad, there may be less commitment on their part to attend, so no-show percentages will be higher.

During the Seminar

Determining how many people you will need to work the event and who they should be is important. The presenters themselves will be kept busy on the day of the event, so staff will need to sign in and greet attendees, answer questions from venue staff and guests, say hello to clients and special guests, make sure the refreshments are ready, and confirm that everything is running smoothly.

When selecting seminar staff, make sure they are comfortable and conversant with the subject being covered so they can handle general questions. Pick people who are outgoing and approachable. Also be certain that the staff knows the layout of the venue, including locations of restrooms, phones, coat check, and other amenities. Conduct a walk-through before the start of the seminar. Assign someone to handle the audio/visual needs, including setting up the laptop and projector, raising and lowering the lights, and cueing slides and videos. When handled properly these details let the audience know that thought and preparation went into all aspects of the presentation. Conversely, lack of preparation—for instance, if the speaker needs to walk to the back of the room to lower and raise the lights—reflects poorly. Make sure all support staff are onsite at least 60 to 90 minutes prior to the start of the seminar.

Depending on the room configuration and the number of attendees, there are several options for the most appropriate seating arrangements:

- Small tables for four. This seating arrangement has proven effective in seminars where clients are invited to bring friends. The client couple can enjoy private conversation with their friends before the seminar begins.
- Tables of six or eight (preferably round tables) for seating people who do not necessarily know one another.
- U-shaped arrangement of tables
- Auditorium or classroom style

Regardless of the style chosen, make sure there is ample walking space and room for display tables, refreshments, and a speakers' area.

The Presentation

The room looks great. The staff is getting attendees into their seats. Now it is up to the presenter to pull it all together and make the attendees grateful they came. The presentation should be delivered in a clear and understandable manner. If slides, overheads, or computer images are used, be sure they are clear and readable from every corner of the room. It is unprofessional to apologize for the readability of a presentation slide. The following guidelines will help ensure a successful talk:

- If you are the one presenting, write out the main points of the presentation in advance and rehearse them with your colleagues. Do not read from a script—you'll put everyone to sleep—but feel free to refer to notes.
- The presentation and the information provided should be genuinely educational. The audience is there to learn—not for a sales pitch.
- The presentation should be made as interactive as possible. Create opportunities for audience participation and encourage questions.
- Limit each slide to one key point. Don't crowd too much information onto one slide. Break up complex information into multiple slides. Estimate one to two slides per minute.
- An audience's attention span is 30 to 45 minutes. Keep presentations within a reasonable time frame.
- Provide attendees with handouts of material related to the seminar topic or a summary of the presentation itself.
- Video or audiotape the presentation and post to your web site and to public sites, such as YouTube. Make sure to include the link in any correspondence with attendees and those unable to attend.

Follow-Up: The Key to Success

It is startling how many seminar leads are never pursued. As with trade shows, some people think that once the event is over, the job is done. Not following up is akin to training for a marathon, running a personal best time, and just before the finish line, pulling up short and walking away. The end of the seminar signals the start of the real work, the stage at which follow-up and selling begins. Initiating a few simple practices will keep the lines of communication open:

- Create a follow-up letter that can be sent to attendees immediately after the seminar.
- Invitees who requested an appointment or additional material should be the highest priority and be contacted within 24 to 48 hours of the seminar.
- Confirmed invitees who were unable to attend should be sent a letter indicating that a follow-up call will be made to answer any questions. Also, send a link to the presentation or other relevant material.

Measuring Results

Return on investment in a seminar is relatively easy to assess. These are the important measurements:

- Cost-per-qualified lead. Divide the overall costs of the seminar (invitations, space, refreshments, staff time, speakers' gifts, handouts) by the number of those who responded (even if they didn't attend). The cost-per-lead should be a metric that you will use to measure other seminar efforts.

- New business. After following up with both attendees and no-shows at least once and preferably three to four times, total the new or additional business generated by these leads. If possible, project this business forward for one to three years.
- ROI. Determine this figure by dividing new business by total cost.

Seminars and trade shows are basic tools of financial marketing. For both large corporations and individual practitioners, they are a common way of building sales through person-to-person, interactive channels. The key to using these tools successfully is in thorough preparation and follow-up. While not costly compared to many marketing tools, seminars and trade shows are time-consuming. Before undertaking these methods, make sure you have the commitment to get the most value from your efforts.

CHAPTER 11

Relationship Marketing

It is far cheaper to retain current customers than to acquire new ones. Relationship marketing not only helps increase customer longevity but also increases customer wallet share. That, in turn, increases loyalty and profitability.

What is relationship marketing? Consider this example: 20 lucky co-workers won $55 million in the Texas Lottery. By the time they had verified their win, it was 2 a.m., but the group decided they did not want to risk losing the ticket. So they called up the president of Texas First Bank, who met them in downtown Texas City along with a lawyer and a justice of the peace. On the hood of a pickup, they drew up an official contract agreement, signed it, and stuffed it with the lottery ticket into the bank's night deposit box.

It's not likely that similar winners could get hold of the president or anyone else at Bank of America or Wells Fargo in the middle of the night. That kind of customized, small-town service doesn't exist much anymore. And yet, the country's largest financial institutions are attempting to provide something like it. Today, it gets fancy names—service marketing or relationship marketing or retention marketing or loyalty marketing but it all means the same thing: Finding a way to keep customers happy so they will stay and grow with your organization.

In a saturated market like financial services, it is extremely important to focus marketing efforts on retaining, cross-selling, and up-selling current customers, in both consumer and institutional markets. Estimates of the cost of retaining customers versus acquiring them vary by factors of five to 10 times or more. By one estimate, there is a 50-fold differential between retention and acquisition value.[1]

Clearly, it is cheaper by orders of magnitude to retain current customers than it is to acquire new ones. Successful cross-sales can help build customer loyalty: The more products customers have, the more likely they will stay with the provider. Up-selling is important because the greater the percentage of total assets a customer has with a given institution (known as *share of wallet*), the greater the profitability of the customer.

What Is Customer Loyalty and Why Does It Matter?

According to Frederick Reichheld, the leading authority on customer loyalty and a professor at the Harvard Business School, "A 5 percent increase in customer retention produces more than a 25 percent increase in profit." Reichheld has also posited that only one question is needed to determine customer loyalty: "How likely are you to recommend our company to a friend or colleague?" This insight has had an impact on the thinking of top managers and the emergence of a "Net Promoter Score" as a baseline for determining customer loyalty.

It seems to work. When JD Power & Associates compared net promoter scores to renewal rates for auto insurance buyers, it found that there was a strong correlation, as shown in Table 11.1.

TABLE 11.1 Promoters Equal Profitability

	Net Promoter*	Actual Retention
USAA	80%	95%
Geico	44%	84%
Industry Average	38%	79%
Progressive	28%	71%
GMAC	25%	69%

*Answered "7" to question, "On a scale of 1-7, how likely are you to recommend this product or service?"

Adapted from JD Power & Associates. Financial Returns from Committed Customers. August 2007.

Why Customer Retention Matters

Before you can grow customer assets, you have to make sure you keep the customers you have. In some sub-segments of the industry, this is not difficult, because customers are virtually locked in. For example, holders of commercial mortgages are hemmed in by prepayment penalties; annuity policyholders generally pay a substantial penalty for early withdrawals. Even in situations where customers can move freely, they generally don't. A private banking client has too much tied up in his banking relationship to change banks because someone offers a better deal. A corporate retirement plan sponsor may put millions of dollars at risk if it changes plan providers. In many cases, the rewards of moving just aren't worth the costs—psychologically or financially.

But that doesn't mean financial marketers can afford to ignore current customers. In some sub-segments of financial services, customer turnover is relatively high. Credit card consumers who carry balances routinely switch to better interest rate offers. In mutual funds, many investors chase returns. It is estimated that turnover among retail mutual fund shareholders and bank checking account holders is around 15 percent annually.[2] Any marketer who can improve on that rate is adding significant value to the bottom line.

FIGURE 11.1 Lifetime Customer Value: The longer Customers Remain, the Greater Their Value

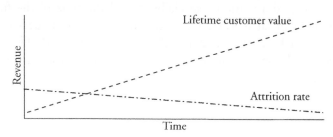

The advantages of retaining current customers go beyond just having one more customer.

The longer the customer's tenure, the more profitable the customer. Customer profitability increases substantially in the second year and thereafter, as purchases rise and expenses associated with servicing new customers decline.

Current customers are the best potential new customers. Cross-selling (selling a new product or service) and up-selling (increasing the investment in the customer's current service) are the most cost-effective ways of generating new business. A happy customer who already does business with you is far more likely to buy more products and services in the future.

Existing customers bring referrals. For many financial companies, most new business may come from referrals by current clients.

The loyalty cycle is important. The more customers do business with you, the more likely they are to remain customers, the more profitable they are likely to be. Lifetime value of customers increases with each product they purchase and each year they remain customers (see Figure 11.1).

Methods of Relationship Building

Building customer relationships involves both customer service and marketing. In most organizations the marketing function does not have a great deal of authority over the service side of the equation. (The exception is situations in which sales and service are combined in one function, such as an independent financial adviser.) But even though service quality may be outside the control of marketing, there are proactive tools marketers can use to improve retention levels.

Onboarding for Newcomers

Like most companies, American Express has found that attrition rates are highest during the first 12 to 18 months after a cardholder has signed on. The company therefore assigns new customers to a special service team. New customers also receive more special offers and attention, especially around the time of the first renewal. Other ways that financial marketers can give new customers special attention is through welcome packages that may include special value-added offers, direct contact information, and a phone call to ensure that the client is satisfied with the activation of the service.

New Customer Experience Program Impacts Bottom Line

Formal onboarding programs have become more common in recent years. A private bank instituted a New Customer Experience package that consisted of more than 11 touch points over the first 120 days:

Referral Thank You Card
New Client Welcome Card
New Client Welcome Package
Account Manager Intro Call to New Client
Client Introduction to Call Center
Online Services Demonstration
Account Set-up Checklist
60-Day Check-in with Client
Investment Statement Review
Client Interest Profile
120 Day Follow-up Call

To measure the effectiveness of the new client onboarding program, the bank compared 210 new clients who went through the New Client Experience process versus 210 new clients who did not (during the same timeframe):

- Clients who went through the onboarding process **increased account balances by 20 percent more** than those who did not go through the process
- Clients who went through the onboarding process **opened 2 to 3 times more accounts/services** than those who did not go through the process
- Of the clients who went through the onboarding process **more than 96 percent were very satisfied** with their initial relationship.

Satisfaction and sales increase with each subsequent contact in the first 60 days—up to seven touches. Multi-touch onboarding also leads to a reduction of attrition of between 2 and 3 percent.

Source: "Distinctive Client Experience" presentation, Financial Services Marketing Conference, 2007.

Pre-emptive Intervention

There are high-risk moments or trigger events that can cause loss of clients. A merger presents one such risk. If clients are going to have to adapt to new systems and new personnel anyway, they figure they might as well examine some of the alternatives. Similarly, an adviser or broker who is changing firms may bring many of her clients along with her. Or a trigger event may occur, such as a customer move to another locality or a need for a financial product not offered by the current provider.

On the institutional side it's even more important to be proactive, since each lost customer has greater value. Client (and sales force) communications should be integrated into transition management. By including the marketing department in transition team meetings, marketing has the information as soon as decisions are made and can then create materials to inform internal staff and clients.

Internal staff should be informed well ahead of public announcements. For example, if there are to be closures or layoffs, communicate this information as quickly as possible so that staff is not left in the dark about their future.

Make sure client representatives are given as much information as is available, and encourage them to share with clients.

Communicate with clients and staff regularly throughout the process. As soon as the merger or transition is announced, send each institutional client a personalized letter from senior management announcing the deal and explaining how it will impact the client. Send out updates to clients and staff outlining the transition process, reporting on progress to date, and answering questions.

Effective Merger Communications

Wells Fargo was quick to establish a blog when it took over Wachovia Bank—even before major decisions had been made. The goal was to communicate, have conversations, create a resource for customers to find information, ask questions, and express concerns in a forum where Wells could be part of customers' conversations and provide appropriate and timely responses.

Wells got a lot of positive online support for acting quickly and for letting customers have their say—positive and negative. Some lessons learned:

- Have real people write the blog in a natural, conversational way (no corporate speak)
- Have a clear focus
- Make it easy to comment
- Listen and respond to comments
- Allow reasonable, negative comments

At-Risk Clients

Many CRM systems can anticipate at-risk clients through metrics that identify anomalous behavior patterns (such as a large withdrawal). An at-risk modeling capacity can send alerts to a contact center or individual for intervention. In one study, rapidly taking proactive steps to keep the customer reduced new account attrition by 50 percent in six months.[3]

Other events also call for proactive intervention:

- Bad publicity (for example, after the bank meltdown of 2008, many customers sought to move to banks they perceived to be "safer")
- Market upheavals
- Personnel changes

Profiting from Service Issues

Service problems are common—and often unavoidable. But a service break does not have to lead to a client loss—in fact, it can be an opportunity to build customer loyalty, if handled well.

One of the most important proactive tools is to create a structured program to intervene when there is a service problem. In some cases, this is done very simply by creating templates for letters of apology or explanation that can be used by the field. Bank marketers may offer branch managers an online letter library with numerous options—from a simple apology to a gift basket. By making amends for inconvenience, financial institutions can actually turn service failures into relationship-building experiences. Satisfying the customer after a service problem actually looms larger than the problem itself in influencing overall customer satisfaction, future purchase intentions, and positive word-of-mouth communications.[4]

Clients who received outstanding recovery after a moderate to severe service break were 10 times more likely to be loyal afterward than if they had never experienced a service break. It is how your organization responds to service problems that makes the difference between losing a customer and gaining a loyal booster.

- Acknowledge the problem
- Determine who is responsible
- Take action to resolve the problem
- Let the client know that action is taking place and the approximate time period until successful resolution
- Once the problem is resolved, make sure the client is satisfied
- For high value clients, make a goodwill gesture—send a note, flowers, or other acknowledgements

Maintain Ongoing Contact

Of course, it is best not to wait until there is a problem before contacting the customer. Some brokerage firms have successfully improved customer value (both retention and up-sell) by having financial advisers schedule monthly phone conferences with their high-value clients. Not only do clients feel they are getting more personal attention, but they often save their questions for the appointed phone conference, thus saving their own and the adviser's time. Metrics have shown that one-to-one contact is the most important factor in retaining a client's business and that the primary reason clients leave is that they haven't been contacted.

As shown in Figure 11.2, less than two contacts a year can put brokerage customers at risk. With three or more contacts, the risk of losing a customer declines substantially.

Frequent and timely communications are important, whether the customers are individuals or institutions. Examples might include newsletters, regularly scheduled e-mails and phone calls, field salespeople calling on clients, open houses, seminars, and other client functions, such as meetings with clients at trade shows and conferences. Even something as basic as an account statement can affect customer loyalty. Upgrading its format to make it easier to understand is a prime retention device.

Client Publications

Client publications, whether printed or online, are valuable for relationship building, since one of their main benefits is to get your company's name in front of the client regularly.

A client newsletter should not be devoted to selling products and services. If the newsletter is perceived only as advertising, it will not be read. There should be editorial content that is of benefit to the reader. For example, a newsletter for small-business clients of Chase offered a service feature in each issue on topics such as time management, simple marketing ideas, or reducing employee theft. Offering charts, checklists, how-to information, important dates, and similar material may inspire the reader to print out the issue and refer to it later.

FIGURE 11.2 Regular Contact Cements Relationships

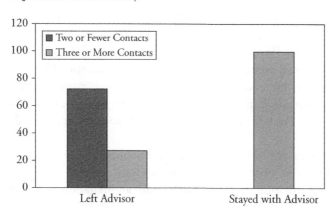

Source: Registered Rep, 2003.

TABLE 11.2   DOs and DON'Ts for Newsletters

DOs	DON'Ts
• Plan the contents of each issue in advance. Include a time line for completion. Get agreement on the topics and the schedule from everyone involved.	• Publish on an irregular schedule. The more frequently and regularly you publish, the more your clients will think about you.
• Make sure content is appropriate for the audience in subject matter, tone (informal versus formal), and level of readability (e.g., mass audience, professional, age-specific).	• Talk down to your readers or use insider jargon if you are trying to reach a general audience. Don't make your newsletter sound like a business report. Use a journalistic model, with a compelling lead paragraph, lots of quotes, and informative examples.
• Feature anyone in your organization who can provide information of value to your readers, such as economists, analysts, and other industry experts.	• Include articles just to massage a higher up's ego—appeal to your readers, not your own organization.
• Use call-outs, sidebars, captions, and other visual elements to direct the reader's attention to important subject matter.	• Assume that the reader will find the "meat" of the story in the fourth paragraph.
• Proofread carefully. Pay particular attention to headlines, call-outs, etc., which are often not spell-checked. And remember that spell-checking won't catch words that are used incorrectly, like "site" for "cite."	• Assume that readers will overlook typos or grammatical mistakes. These reflect badly on your brand.

When planning your first issue, aim for regularly scheduled features. This makes it easier to come up with story ideas. For example, a newsletter for prime brokerage clients might have regular updates on operations, technology, and legal issues, and a question-and-answer column explaining electronic features. A newsletter for high-net-worth property insurance clients can feature a regular column on antiques and collectibles, another on insurance news items, and another on how to mitigate risks.

Loyalty Programs

One of the most brilliant marketing ideas ever dreamed up was to emboss a year after the words "Member since . . ." onto the American Express (AmEx) card. Membership is central to the American Express brand, and that message is reinforced by its taglines ("Membership has its Privileges" "Membership Rewards®"), its advertising, its merchandising, and special events. AmEx has created such a sense of loyalty that customers are willing to pay more for the privilege of being higher-level members. There are several tiers of American Express cards, each charging different annual "dues," with a corresponding increase in benefits and a perceived elevation in personal status for the cardholder.

AmEx members are so loyal, in fact, that members were willing to join a card level that didn't even exist. For years, there were rumors about the mysterious (and nonexistent) American Express "black" card, an invitation-only card reserved for the upper-most tier. Since AmEx couldn't quash the rumors, it decided to make them true—and issued a black Centurion card in 1999. The company found that many of its most loyal customers wanted the card—and were willing to pay a $5000 initiation fee and $2500 per year for the privilege.

Few companies have developed the level of customer loyalty that AmEx and its long-time agency, Ogilvy & Mather, managed to cultivate over many years. But many try. Credit card issuers, in particular, have developed loyalty programs that involve rewards for purchases. Once the customer has built up a certain level of rewards, the cost of leaving is high. If your customer has 50,000 points saved up, she will be reluctant to give up your card, even if she has to pay a higher annual fee. The downside with any loyalty program is that competitors soon match whatever you're offering.

Loyalty programs are expensive to set up and manage. Formal programs make the most sense when a product or service is essentially a commodity—for example, securities trading. Soft-dollar services are essentially a kind of loyalty marketing, as investors get "credits" toward free research or other services in exchange for trading commissions. Another example is prime brokerage, where a hedge fund manager gets low-cost or free office space and other services in exchange for its trading business. Whether on the consumer or institutional side, there are several steps to creating and managing a useful loyalty program.

Branding the program. The program should conform to the company's overall brand image but create a sense of a separate, more privileged "club" of special clients. This may involve a separate logo and/or tagline.

Membership package. You need to let your customers know that they are now members of the "club." A welcome letter is a must—a welcome kit is even better. The kit can contain information about "club" benefits, a newsletter, perhaps a membership card, and a premium designed to reinforce the brand message. For example, a mortgage-development program directed to realtors could offer information on a DVD or a downloadable app to help them prequalify home buyers. Unless your members have specifically asked to join, they probably won't realize they're members of the club unless there is a strong welcome package and ongoing follow-up.

Teaming up for added awareness and benefits. Gain the goodwill of clients by aligning with charitable partners. If your card supports the Audubon Society, include Audubon information, a bird-themed calendar, and other related items. A small business-oriented program, for example, might benefit the local chamber of commerce or offer scholarships to community college students aiming for business careers.

Referral rewards. Referrals are your best source of high-value new customers, and who better to give a referral than a satisfied, current customer? Referral rewards should be built into the program. For example, if the program involves donations to charity, a referral would generate an additional donation, perhaps with an acknowledging gift from the charity in return. Or a referral program could offer better pricing on products or fees, or additional services.

Asking for Referrals

Asking for referrals is difficult for many practitioners. Certain best practices can help keep the referral engine running smoothly.

Who to Ask?

Not all clients are open to giving referrals. If possible, try to segment your clients into the following psychographic types, based on the strength of their relationship with you and their willingness to make referrals (see Figure 11.3).

FIGURE 11.3   Referral Matrix

	Strong Relationship	Weak Relationship
High Willingness	Promoters	Connectors
Low Willingness	Privacy Seekers	Avoiders

Source: Based on research published in "Referrals Revisited," *Investment Advisor,* December 2007.

- Promoters. These are usually outgoing individuals who enjoy sharing their discoveries—on Twitter, with business colleagues, at group events. They are your most loyal and willing clients and should be cultivated. Acknowledge their efforts and thank them in big and small ways.
- Connectors. Like promoters, this group enjoys sharing what it knows. Unfortunately, they may bring you inappropriate referrals. These well-meaning types need to be educated on your capabilities and ideal client profiles, so that they do not waste their time—and yours.
- Privacy seekers. This group is loyal but reluctant to make referrals. They do not naturally share their positive experiences with others and may be unwilling to give out names. However, their referrals can be cultivated in more subtle ways.
- Avoiders neither care nor share. Don't waste your time trying to cultivate referrals from this group.

When to Ask

- Following successful on-boarding
- After successful resolution of a service break
- During a face-to-face meeting
- After expanding the relationship through new or additional services

How to Ask

- Invite the client to bring a guest to a client appreciation event
- Invite the client to lunch along with one of his/her centers of influence
- Include a pass-along copy of white papers, newsletters, and other material
- Make it easy for your clients—ask for referrals to those with a similar profile. For example, if the client is a partner in a legal practice, ask for referrals to other legal professionals.

Once the Client Makes a Referral

- Send a personalized thank you
- Keep the client informed of the outcome of the referral

Special events. Another way to make loyal customers feel special is to invite them to special events. At one time, Chase's Small Business area had a special program for accountants. Among other benefits, accountants were invited to bring their clients to seminars of special interest to small-business owners. Not only did this allow the accountants to build stronger relationships with their own clients, but it also introduced new prospects to Chase in a low-key way, with an implied endorsement from their accountant. On the institutional side, special events to entertain top clients are commonplace and range from corporate skyboxes at the Super Bowl to lunch at one's club.

Large financial companies spend tens of millions of dollars on automated customer relationship management (CRM) systems that they hope will give them a competitive edge. Yet, in many cases, as institutions get large enough to afford these massive data-manipulation systems, they get further from their customers. As the banking industry, for example, becomes more and more concentrated, the megabanks often lose market share to smaller banks. Why? Because smaller banks can offer personalized service that the megabanks can only approximate.

Relationship marketing can work for big companies—just look at American Express. But it will take more than "event-triggering" or "loss-based predictive modeling" to create a company that customers love. It requires staff training up and down the corporate ladder, solid and sustained management commitment, the ability to track and measure service performance, and rewards for service excellence. Lots of financial companies give lip service to these factors, but ask yourself this: Which bank would you have chosen if you had won the lottery?

Notes

1. "Using Customer Analytics to Improve Customer Retention," *Bank Accounting and Finance*, April-May, 2009.
2. "Practical Perspectives," Investment Company Institute annual meeting, May 22, 2003; F. F. Reichheld and W. B. Sasser, "Zero Defections: Quality Comes to Services," *Harvard Business Review*, September-October 1990, 105–111; Cindy Claycomb and Charles L. Martin, "Building Customer Relationships: An Inventory of Service Providers' Objectives and Practices," *Journal of Services Marketing*, 16, 7, 2002.
3. Gartner Group, "Financial Services Marketing: Moving from Push to Pull," presentation by Kimberly Collins Ph.D. to the American Marketing Association, March 2003.
4. R. A. Spreng et al., "Service Recovery: Impact on Satisfaction and Intentions," *Journal of Services Marketing*, 1995, 15–23. Cited in Claycomb, "Building Customer Relationships."

Conclusion

Despite the technological upheavals of the twenty-first century, the financial services industry remains one of American industry's least sophisticated marketers. When the Medici conducted banking business with the pope in the 14th and 15th centuries, they used personal contacts and reputation to generate deals. The investment-banking industry still operates pretty much the same way. True, certain segments of the financial industry have been marketing innovators; banks, for example, were among the first to adopt customer relationship management (CRM) systems to track customer behavior. Nevertheless, a large portion of the industry is only beginning to move from a sales model to a marketing model—a move consumer products manufacturers made in the 1950s.

Ironically, as the old-fashioned relationship-driven businesses, such as investment bankers, wholesale bankers, and brokers and financial advisers, adopt technology and centralized management, sophisticated direct marketers, such as credit card issuers and direct life insurers, are going the other way. The hottest concepts in marketing today are one-to-one marketing and relationship management. Today's state-of-the-art marketing organizations are using statistical modeling and other technology-based processes to replicate the old fashioned one-to-one, relationship-based methods.

Relationship marketing is not the only thing that's regaining popularity. Banks, which started out as retailers, are rediscovering merchandising and display. Institutions like Umpqua Bank and TD Bank are successfully modeling their branches along the lines of Starbucks and Wal-Mart to lure customers inside. Word-of-mouth—now, trendily, called viral marketing—is what all businesses are founded on: Doing a good job so people will say good things about you to other people. In the Internet age, the process can perhaps be accelerated, but Wall Street has always been a rumor mill. No doubt buyers and sellers were gossiping about who was doing what back in the days when the New York Stock Exchange met under a buttonwood tree.

The issues of most pressing concern to financial marketers today are not really new; they're just appearing in new guises. Branding, for example, is the updated version of building a quality reputation. Attempts to build bridges between sales and marketing have been practiced since the days when managers in the home office visited regional branches to "buck up the troops." Concerns about "metrics"—or how to quantify return on marketing investment—date back at least to nineteenth-century merchant John Wanamaker's quip about not knowing which half of his advertising dollars was being wasted. Even the latest rounds of financial market scandals are mere echoes of the past. The Congressional investigations and new banking laws that resulted from the crash of 2008 had their antecedents in the crash of 1929.

What Goes Around, Comes Around

The financial services category encompasses a range of marketing methods and levels of sophistication. One-to-one selling, which many would regard as "old-fashioned," is still the marketing method of choice for most institutional sales, such as pension plan providers and investment bankers. If one looks at the financial services marketplace as a continuum, with personal relationship selling at one end and the use of technology at the other, then institutional sales would be the most personal and least technological. Other face-to-face sellers include personal financial advisors and most commissioned salespeople.

At the other end of spectrum, credit card issuers and other direct marketers use the most sophisticated, modeling-based methods. Most direct marketers never interact personally with their customers; instead, they are attempting to emulate personal relationships through CRM and machine-created personalization. For example, a web site might use programming that recognizes a customer, greets her by name, and offers suggestions based on past behavior. The paradox is that as marketers move further from the actual customers, they are at the same time attempting to recapture the type of one-to-one relationship that institutional salespeople still maintain with their clients.

Banks and other top-down marketers occupy a middle position. They have moved away from the one-to-one personal relationship model as they pushed clients to non-branch channels such as automated teller machines (ATMs) and the Internet. But now, using technology, they are moving toward "virtual personal relationships" through such means as online customer service that can be activated during online transactions to connect customers with real people.

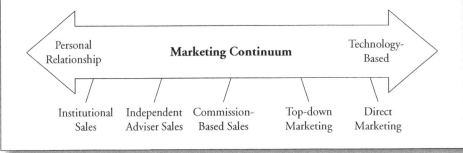

None of this is meant to suggest that financial professionals have little to learn about marketing. Unlike marketers in many other industries, many financial services marketers come from elsewhere—either a different industry or a different position in financial services. When one moves from the trading floor or sales force to a marketing position, the product knowledge is there, but there may not be a lot of marketing know-how. On the other hand, the increasingly common career route that leads from a consumer products company to a financial services company is not sufficient preparation for the industry-specific challenges that must be faced. Even those with marketing experience in, say, mutual funds, face a steep learning curve when moving into the altogether differently regulated world of hedge funds.

Large financial organizations are often accused of not communicating across the "silos" represented by their various operations and departments, and there are even greater apparent gulfs between banking and brokerage, money management and trading, insurance and credit cards, and all the rest. Despite these differences within the financial sub-segments, financial marketers can learn from one another. A successful e-marketing campaign by a mutual fund company can inspire a personal financial planner or a wholesale banker.

The reader will have noticed that there is very little in this book about financial services practices outside the United States. Americans can learn much from other business cultures and, in fact, financial-marketing theory and practice often appear to be more advanced in Europe and Asia than in the United States. But given the size of the U.S. financial industry and its international prominence, it seemed sensible to start here. We have attempted to give an overview of current practice, provide a guide for students and practitioners, and start a conversation about next steps.

We welcome your comments and suggestions, case studies, and questions. Our blog, (www.fsmhandbook.com.), will be continually updated with new case studies and more information on subjects that could only be touched on here. We look forward to engaging with our professional colleagues.

Appendix

Applying Marketing Principles to Sales Practice

Building Your Plan
   Segment Your Markets
   Set Goals
   Prioritize Tactics Against Goals and Resources
   Measure Results

Practice Examples
   Segmentation in Practice
      Segmentation Expands a Salesperson's Practice
      A Wholesaler Prioritizes Segments
      Additional Segmentation by Bank District
      A Start-Up Independent Financial Adviser Selects Target Segments

   Positioning in Practice
      Establishing a Reputation and Differentiating a Practice
      Positioning within a Larger Firm
      Sub-Branding and Co-Branding a Local Market Initiative
      Positioning a Start-Up

   The Market Plan in Practice
      Building a Plan
      A Formal Plan
      Buy-In on the Market Plan
      A Plan for an Independent

   Advertising in Practice
      Determining When Advertising Is Appropriate
      Advertising for Corporate Buyers
      Local Advertising
      A First Ad

   Public Relations in Practice
      Getting Out the Word About The Women's Planning Group
      Institutional PR
      Generating Publicity for the SAIF Program
      A Public Relations Investment Pays Off

160

Conclusion

This appendix is devoted exclusively to the sales professional—whether you sell to consumers or institutions, whether you are independent or receive compensation from a brokerage, insurance company, or other financial services organization. This special section is designed to help you focus on how the marketing strategies and tactics described elsewhere in this book can improve your sales effectiveness.

To help you translate the principles of marketing into sales practice, we have provided four examples of real-life sales situations that are threaded throughout the rest of the appendix.

Anyone who makes a living by persuading other people to buy something needs to understand what marketing is. Marketing is the process of planning who you are selling to, what you are selling them, and then choosing the tactics that will best achieve your goals—from personal sales calls, seminar selling, or inviting clients to a golf outing to direct mail, public relations, and social media.

Many sales professionals are great champions of planning—for their clients. If you sell financial advisory or consulting services, you've no doubt talked to your clients about the importance of having a road map to achieve financial goals. But do you have as good a map for your own business goals?

Market planning takes time—something most sales professionals cannot spare. But consider whether it is worth taking a few hours to ensure a steady stream of new prospects, month after month, in all markets. A market plan doesn't have to be elaborate. Even the most basic market plan can help improve your sales success in numerous ways:

- **Increase profitability.** Like most businesses, you probably derive 80 percent of your profit from 20 percent of your clients. But are you allocating your time to reflect that? Are you getting the most from your best clients? Could you get more—share of wallet, referrals, longer retention? How do you get more clients who resemble that highly profitable 20 percent? A marketing plan helps you apportion your time and budget to make sure you are targeting the highest-value clients and prospects.
- **Save time and money.** "Seat of the pants" marketing is inefficient. If you respond to opportunities as they come up—buying an ad in the journal of an organization because a friend is a member, or joining a chamber of commerce to develop contacts—you may or may not achieve results. But even if you do get new business, how do the results compare to other tactics you might have chosen? Your marketing plan sets your objectives, provides a road map, and lets you measure results. A plan doesn't prevent you from taking advantage of one-off opportunities, but it will tell you at every stage whether these opportunities are suitable for your goals.
- **Work better as a team.** As more companies create a team-based approach to selling, market planning is a way to get input and buy-in from everyone on the team, to make sure each person knows what is expected, and to align all sales efforts against a common set of objectives.
- **Build better relationships with clients.** Most financial sales organizations have shifted focus away from generating transactions toward building relationships. Selling is no longer about "eating what you kill." It's about understanding client needs and finding appropriate ways to meet those needs. From a marketing perspective, relationship-building is less about acquiring new customers and more about retaining and increasing business with the clients you already have. Better relationships generate more referral business.
- **Determine what works.** Many salespeople use the same tactics repeatedly: a client lunch at the country club, trade shows, building alliances with other professionals. While these approaches may work, there may be others that could bring bigger results with fewer resources. Successful marketing depends on measuring the results of every campaign and using those metrics to make every dollar work harder.

Building Your Plan

A formal market plan can be a 20-page document or a two-page spreadsheet.

There are many extras that can strengthen a plan, but there are only four essential elements for a successful plan.

No. 1: Segment Your Markets

Every plan should focus on a few well-defined segments, including the following:

- Your current clients. Your current clients are always your best prospects. You need to identify specific goals, such as generating more income per client, increasing the percentage of clients' assets, or increasing the number of clients who contribute the most to your bottom line.
- Those who resemble your top clients. For example, the top 20 percent of your clients may be mostly entrepreneurs, or golfers, or people who drive Mercedes—or all three. Find as many common elements among your top group as you can. This will help you develop specific marketing tactics (such as a joint program with your local Mercedes dealership).
- Expand your client base. If your client base is maturing or you're in a competitive market, explore the potential of a new target segment. Is everyone pursuing doctors? How about hospital administrators or pharmaceutical sales executives?

No. 2: Set Goals

For each of your target market segments, you need to set measurable goals that are meaningful for your practice. For example, for a new target segment, a set of objective goals might look like this:

Segment: Pharmaceutical Sales Executives with Incomes more than $250,000

	1-year goal	2-year goal
Number of new clients from segment	4	12
Average account size	$150,000	$350,000
"Wallet share" per account	40%	60%

No. 3: Prioritize Tactics Against Goals and Resources

There are many marketing tactics—from advertising to social media, from seminars to referral-building techniques. Go back to your goals and list all of the tactics that might be effective in reaching them. For example, penetrating a new market segment can be accomplished through LinkedIn contacts, advertising, seminars, or public relations.

Brainstorming potential acquisition and expansion tactics can be fun and creative, and should include your whole team. When you've finished, list all the potential tactics you've come up with. Assign each a score, based on its cost, the human resources required, and the likelihood that the tactic will result in a positive return. The following chart shows an example of the results of such a brainstorming session, based on pharmaceutical sales executives.

	Out-of-pocket cost	Total staff hours/year	Estimated return*	Score
Join their professional organizations	$500	30	5:1	A
Develop opportunities to speak to their groups	$0	20	6:1	A
Sponsor charitable event	$5,000	30	4:1	B
Advertise in their group publication	$15,000	15	3:1	C
Seminars	$20,000	120	5:1	C

*Estimated return can be a ratio (i.e., 2:1 = $2 in potential new business for every dollar spent) or another metric meaningful to your business.

This example demonstrates that a rather simple tactical plan can clearly show where you are most likely to get the best return for your marketing dollars and staff resources. Allocating your budget against your priorities will help you avoid wasting money on items that have low potential.

No. 4: Measure Results

The first time you lay out your plan, there will be some guesswork involved. Will tactic "X" really return five to one on your investment? How much new money is that anyway? How many new accounts? Did that match your estimates?

To answer such questions, you must measure your results against your expectations. Tactic A didn't work as planned? Don't do it again. Or try doing it a different way. Tactic B took longer and cost more, but still performed well. Perhaps you should re-prioritize.

Measuring the results of your marketing plan is no different than evaluating a portfolio strategy. If your plan didn't help you reach your goals, change it.

Practice Examples

The four examples that follow are meant to cover a range of financial sales situations. Inez G. (IG) runs an Insurance Group. She's a top producer and sales manager of her own agency. Her group is affiliated with a national insurance company, but Inez and her employees have a good degree of autonomy in marketing matters, with complete responsibility for their own profitability.

Ron W. (RW) is a Retirement Wholesaler who works for a mutual fund company and is a wholesaler of defined contribution plans. His market is wire house financial advisers, so his marketing mission is twofold: selling these advisers on his own product, and helping the advisers sell to their clients.

Bonnie-Dee M. (BDM) is a Bank District Manager. Bonnie-Dee's markets are her branch managers, their staff, and their customers. While Bonnie-Dee must work within the bank's overall marketing structure, she can authorize marketing initiatives that will drive more business to the branches.

Frank A. (FA) is just starting an independent Financial Advisory practice after working for many years as a commissioned broker. His example is designed to mirror the issues faced by those who are relatively new to marketing, but it should prove helpful to anyone who is dealing with a particular business situation (such as creating an interactive campaign) for the first time.

Each example illustrates how the lessons learned in the body of the book are applied in the real world. It may be helpful to refer to the corresponding chapter when reviewing the sales examples.

KEY

IG = Inez G. = Insurance Group
RW = Ron W. = Retirement Wholesaler
BDM = Bonnie-Dee M. = Bank District Manager
FA = Frank A. = Financial Adviser

Segmentation in Practice

This section refers to material discussed in Chapter 1.

IG. Segmentation Expands a Salesperson's Practice

Inez G., a top producer for a major insurance company, has grown her practice in Chicago over the years, and she now has five agents on her team. Her group focuses primarily on women business owners. Two members of her group, who were formerly in pharmaceutical sales, concentrate on the planning needs of nurses, nurse practitioners, and physician's assistants. Further, through market research and her own experience, Inez knows that a growing number of Hispanic women are starting their own businesses. Inez reached out to the local Hispanic chamber of commerce and began reading the local and national Hispanic business publications. Through word-of-mouth and networking, Inez initiated an aggressive campaign to recruit Hispanic agents who could devote their efforts exclusively to this growing and valuable market.

RW. A Wholesaler Prioritizes Segments

Ron W. is a wholesaler for a national mutual fund company, specializing in defined contribution retirement plans. His market consists of wire house brokers in six states in the Southwest. His employer provides marketing, sales, and product support, but Ron is the primary driver of business initiatives in his region.

Ron's territory includes more than 5,000 individuals who are potential retailers of National Mutual Fund Company's product. Ron has prioritized his total market into several sub-segments, as outlined below:

- By current status. Because he has limited time to sell and service his clients, Ron has assigned one of two status levels to each current and prospective account: A status includes the top 20 percent of current accounts and "hot" prospects. These are individuals who have large books of business with Ron's competitors and who have indicated an interest in adding NMFC's product to their offerings. Ron devotes 80 percent of his time to his A list.
- By sales potential. Although 80 percent of his current clients are therefore in the B category, some have more potential value than others. Ron is attempting to analyze the potential for sales among those B clients who may be doing business with competitors. Another B group includes "warm" prospects who have indicated interest in NMFC's product but whose potential value is unknown.
- By strength of relationship. Ron is well known among his A list clients and well regarded by most of them. However, he has to compete for recognition with B list clients and A and B list prospects. So he will need to develop relationship-building tactics that will highlight his retirement services expertise and his ability to help his target brokers increase their sales.

BDM. Additional Segmentation by Bank District

Bonnie-Dee M. is the district manager for the Alligator Banking Corporation Bank (ABC Bank), a mid-size bank with branches throughout Florida and Georgia. Bonnie-Dee is responsible for 40 branches in southeastern Florida.

Even though ABC Bank has sophisticated segmentation metrics, derived from its customer relationship management (CRM) data, it encourages local districts to customize programs for their particular demographic segments. In South Florida, that meant the elderly. Nearly 40 percent of ABC Bank's customers in Dade, Broward, and Palm Beach counties are 65 or older.

FA. A Start-Up Independent Financial Adviser Selects Target Segments

Frank A. is 33 years old, married, with a three-year-old child and another on the way. He lives in a leafy suburb outside of Philadelphia. After receiving a BA in economics and an MBA in finance, he joined a large brokerage firm as an account executive, where he built a sizable book of business. But changes in the firm's commission structure and lack of control over client service made him realize his prospects for growth at the firm were limited. With a small nest egg that he hoped would carry him through, Frank left his commissioned sales position and became an independent financial adviser.

Although several of Frank's best clients made the move with him, Frank knew that he needed to start moving more prospects into his pipeline. It can take months, or even years, to convert prospects into clients, so Frank needed to continually develop new leads.

Instead of looking for "everyone" to target, Frank realized he needed to focus on specific client segments. By taking a narrow focus, he was not eliminating prospects— he was putting his limited resources behind the most viable prospects.

Many of Frank's clients from his former job had been families in his town. Several of them had come from his church and his country club. In fact, Frank's clients very much resembled Frank.

Therefore, Frank thought it made sense to begin with his own geo-demographics and those of his former clients. Typically they were married couples, 30 to 45 years old, living within 20 miles of his town, who owned a home and had at least one child. They would belong to organizations similar to his church and country club.

Targeting a market segment he knew well was a real advantage for Frank, because he already had a lot of information about his chosen segment. Because he travels in these circles, he knows which local publications these potential clients read, where to find them on Sunday afternoons (on the golf course or at the kids' soccer practice). He knows, with a pretty high degree of accuracy, their incomes, education, and the value of their homes. He knows their aspirations for their futures and for their children's futures.

Frank bolstered this knowledge with solid online research as well as conversations with "centers of influence." He found census data about his community and identi- fied the zip codes with the highest potential. He researched the names of business and social organizations, church groups, and civic groups, and he contacted friends and business leaders to provide him with company and organizational lists that might be useful in his prospecting efforts.

Looking for parents with elementary-school-age children, he compiled lists from PTA directories of elementary schools in the target zip codes, and even used online access to old issues of the newspaper to find old birth announcements. From all this research, Frank compiled a list of names of families in his targeted demographics. He would use these for online and mail campaigns (see the section on "Interactive Marketing in Practice" later in this appendix).

His best prospecting tools, he felt, were his church and country club membership directories. Since he knew most of the members by name, he could judge whether they fit into his target segments and whether they lived in his targeted zip codes. Based on his chosen demographics, he winnowed these two lists down to the families who best fit his target segment. Frank would focus on getting referrals to these names first.

Positioning in Practice

This section refers to material discussed in Chapter 2.

IG. Establishing a Reputation and Differentiating a Practice

Early in her career Inez G. realized that she couldn't be all things to all people, so she focused on meeting the insurance and financial planning needs of women busi- ness owners. She established and began marketing herself under her own "doing-busi- ness-as" name, or DBA, which she named the Women's Planning Group (WPG).

She created brochures and a web site geared specifically toward women, held seminars on topics important to women business owners, and coordinated business-card exchanges to help women network and meet other female business owners. She also became active in local chapters of women's organizations, including the National Association for Female Executives (NAFE) and the National Association of Women Business Owners (NAWBO). Her involvement helped her grow her business, and at the same time positioned her and her agents as positive forces and role models among women business owners. Inez now has three agents supporting the women's business market and two agents focused on female medical practitioners. She and her team are now exploring opportunities among female Hispanic business owners that she identified in her segmentation process.

RW. Positioning within a Larger Firm

Because Ron works for a nationally recognized mutual fund wholesaler, he does not need to develop a look or image of his own. However, he does have to position himself and his firm within his broker market. He noticed that many of the brokers he works with have complained that Ron's home office is bureaucratic and takes too long to answer inquiries or create proposals. Therefore, Ron's positioning strategy will involve countering the negatives of his parent company with his own exceptional level of service. He has developed a mission statement that states:

- I am reachable by phone or e-mail 24/7
- Every call or e-mail will be returned within 24 hours or less
- Every open inquiry will get a weekly status update

Most important, Ron is faithful to these statements. His client brokers know that they can rely on him to service their accounts, resolve issues with the home office, and make sure that sales are credited promptly.

BDM. Sub-Branding and Co-Branding a Local Market Initiative

ABC Bank had developed a Silver Assets program for its customers over age 50. It included free checking, free MasterCard or Visa, preferred rates on home equity loans, preferred rates on certificates of deposit, and a reverse mortgage program. The Silver Assets program was widely advertised in newspapers in Miami, Fort Lauderdale, Boca Raton, and West Palm Beach.

Bonnie-Dee decided that her district would go one step beyond the Silver Assets program and institute a breakfast seminar series on investing for retirees. She decided, with corporate approval, to sub-brand the new initiative, and she held a contest among the branches to come up with a name. The winner was Silver Assets Investment Focus—SAIF—pronounced "safe." The name was easy to remember, lent itself to brand extensions (see the discussion on SAIF Harbor in the "Relationship Marketing in Practice" section), and conveyed the positive attribute of safety.

There were several advantages to creating these seminars: (1) They would bring customers into the branches, along with friends and family (possible referrals), and prospects. (2) ABC Bank branches in the South Florida district had a very low level of market share in investment products. The bank's primary rivals for investment assets are national and local brokerage and financial advisory firms. The seminars would position the bank as a source of financial planning expertise. (3) The program could be co-branded with community organizations. This would be a win-win, because the bank would get recognition for its support, and the organizations would get financial backing for their activities. It could also boost ABC Bank's commercial business with these local nonprofit organizations.

FA. Positioning a Start-Up

When Frank started his business, the first thing he did after filing the necessary business papers was to order personalized business cards, letterheads, and envelopes. His card read "Frank Aldrich, Financial Adviser." He went for an upscale look, black and dark-red inks on cream-colored paper.

To establish his company's image, Frank needed to answer these four questions:

1. What values and attitudes about your company would you want to convey to your constituencies? Think of three adjectives that describe your most important qualities.
2. What are your major strengths?
3. Who are your major competitors?
4. What factors differentiate you from your competition?

For his three adjectives, Frank chose knowledgeable, empathetic, and high quality. What he hoped to convey by the word "knowledgeable" was that he had been in the financial advisory business for many years, kept up with changes and new ideas, and offered a high level of expertise. By "empathetic," he meant he listened to his clients and explored their situations and needs with them to help them find suitable solutions. By "high-quality," Frank was referring not just to the quality of his advice, but also to the quality of his service, his employees (when he had some), and everything else concerning his business.

For his strengths, Frank identified:

- Experience—years in business, advanced degrees
- Personality traits—finds it easy to talk and meet people, good listener
- High standards of performance and integrity

Frank wished to further differentiate from his competitors, by providing a type of expertise that would appeal to his target segments (parents of young children) and fit with his skills. Since he was actively investing for his children's education, he felt this was a good area to pursue as a specialty. Investing for college costs was not the only service he offered, but it would be a good door opener for discussion.

There were several other independent advisers in his geographic region, along with the offices of several national brokerage firms. Frank outlined his strengths and weaknesses by evaluating himself against his competitors. Frank began by listing his strengths—the areas where he thought he was superior in knowledge, communications skills, and professionalism.

Frank's strengths	Adviser 1	Adviser 2	National firms
Experience	= to Frank	> Frank	< Frank
College funding expertise	No experience	No experience	< Frank
Communications skills	= Frank	< Frank	= Frank
Professionalism	= Frank	= Frank	= or < Frank

He then evaluated his competitors on these variables. For example, Adviser 1 had as much experience as Frank but had no particular knowledge of college funding. Adviser 2 had more experience, but poor communications skills. This exercise made it plain to Frank that he had qualities that differentiated him from the competition. In particular, he had no peer in college funding expertise and would emphasize this and his other strengths in his communications material.

The Market Plan in Practice

This section refers to material discussed in Chapter 3.

1G. Building a Plan

Until recently, Inez did not have a formal market plan. Nevertheless, she had built her business systematically by gathering demographic information and conducting research concerning female business owners in Chicago. She contacted leading women's business organizations and created lists of leading women in the community with whom she hoped to cultivate relationships. She joined online groups and worked her alumni association network. Most of her marketing efforts were focused on networking. Occasionally, she would try something new—for example, a public relations (PR) agency contacted her about sending out several press releases on her behalf. She agreed to a three-month trial for $2,000 and did get one local television interview as a result. But she did not get any new business from the news appearance, so she decided not to renew until she had a well-thought-out marketing plan in place.

Now that she has five salespeople working for her, Inez needs a more formal approach to market planning so that everyone knows what their assigned tasks are and everyone is working toward common goals. She meets with her group four times a year to brainstorm tactics. Inez determines her budget based on a percentage of her sales and then prioritizes sales tactics based on cost and potential return. Staff members volunteer to carry out initiatives, or Inez assigns tasks to the most appropriate person.

For example, Carla, who was in pharmaceutical sales, wants to set up in-hospital seminars for her target health-care clients. Carla will contact the hospital administration to make the arrangements and be responsible for creating the event and tracking the results, but everyone on Inez's staff will participate in making the seminar a success.

Other tactics that Inez has decided to try out in the coming quarter include some limited advertising, some co-op arrangements with her home office, and possibly a local sponsorship. She also gave more thought to the role of PR.

RW. A Formal Plan

Unlike Inez and Frank, Ron works for a large corporation, so he does not have total control over his plan. Once a year, in September, National Mutual Fund Company requires Ron to submit results from his current year and estimate next year's goals. These are the data that Ron is asked to provide for his sales territory.

TOTAL NUMBER OF BROKERS SELLING NMFC 401(K) PLANS
- Percentage change for each of the previous three years
- Projected number for the next three years

DOLLAR REVENUES OF NMFC PRODUCTS IN CURRENT YEAR
- Percentage revenue change for each of the previous three years
- Projected revenues for the next three years

ESTIMATED MARKET SHARE IN CURRENT YEAR
- Increase/decrease in market share for each of the previous three years
- Projected increase/decrease over next three years

Ron also has to indicate any local factors that may affect his projections, such as new competitors entering his territory, the impact of national initiatives, and business conditions in the territory.

In addition, Ron must create a marketing budget for the forthcoming year. Using his current year's budget, Ron estimates how much of his revenue was attributable to a given tactic (such as trade advertising, trade shows, and relationship-building). For example, he spent $50,000 on seminars and can trace $15 million in new assets under management (AUM) to these seminars

To propose next year's budget, Ron allocates his prior year's budget according to the return on last year's investment. Since seminars were a big success, he allocates a larger portion of his budget for them in the coming year.

After he has submitted his plan, the home office will assign new goals and budget. In past years, these have been pretty close to what Ron requested.

BDM. Buy-In on the Market Plan

Bonnie-Dee asked each of the 40 branch managers in her district to create a market plan for the Silver Assets Investment Focus (SAIF) program. She asked them to report on the following for their branches:

Customers

- Current investment assets among customers age 60 or older
- Estimate of ABC Bank's market share of investment assets in this group
- Total investment assets held by this group

Non-customers

- Total market potential in number of customers and dollar size of assets

From these data, Bonnie-Dee will establish sales goals for the district. She also asked the branch managers to supply her with information she needed to establish a budget:

- Number of registered investment sales reps in each branch (some branches share reps)
- Suggestions for locations to hold monthly breakfast meetings and estimated costs, including room rental, food, and service
- Estimate of number who would attend each breakfast meeting
- Other expenses to make the seminars a success, including advertising, direct mail, signage, possible gifts, and staff resources

In addition, Bonnie-Dee asked for a SWOT (Strengths, Weaknesses, Opportunities, Threats) analysis (conditions in each branch that could influence the success of the program) and a competitive assessment (what were competitors doing that was similar, and how could ABC Bank do it better).

Once Bonnie-Dee had all the data, she put together a preliminary plan, setting out budget and goals for each branch. She reserved a portion of the budget for the branches to allocate as they chose, with her approval. At a regularly scheduled meeting of all branch managers, Bonnie-Dee presented the preliminary plan and opened it to discussion. After the plan was revised, the branch managers presented it to their sales staff for comments and additional revisions. Once Bonnie-Dee received the final plans back from the branches, she submitted them to her senior management for approval.

FA. A Plan for an Independent

Before creating a formal market plan, Frank had already identified his target market as people like himself—married couples, aged 30 to 45, homeowners, with at least one child. He also decided to position himself as an expert in two areas: education funding and financial planning. He was passionate about the need to plan ahead for financing education since he had had to work nights and weekends to pay his way through college and graduate school. He also believed that almost everyone needed to take the time to develop a financial plan. People needed a road map, he thought, not unlike his own marketing plan.

For his market plan, Frank evaluated his own strengths and weaknesses, his competition, and the opportunities and threats in his environment.

Frank's SWOT analysis

Strengths

Well known and respected in his community
Strong sales and customer relations experience
Subject expertise (college planning)
Active in church group and country club
Base of clients
Marketing support available through wholesalers

Weaknesses

Start-up—not yet known in community
Well-established competition
Identified with his former firm
Limited budget for promotion

Opportunities

Demographic: mini—baby boom in community
Technology: ability to perform sophisticated financial analysis on his laptop
Regulatory: licensing requirements a barrier to entry for new competitors
Economy: market downturn—people are looking for safe investments
Political: Wall Street scandals making independent advisers more attractive

Threats

Economy: Market downturn—people afraid to invest
Economy: Layoffs may lead to more brokers becoming independent competition

Frank's Competitive Analysis

	Frank	Local Independents	National Brokers
Size of marketing budget	Small	Moderate	Large
Target segments (asset size)	$150,000+	$250,000+	$500,000+
Target demographics	30-something	50+	50+
Unique selling advantage	Focus on college funding	Established	National reputation
Key marketing tactics	Public relations	Seminars	National advertising

Marketing objectives

	Months 1–6	Months 7–12	Year 2
Number of qualified new prospects	12	24	75
Number of new clients	4	12	35
Number of retained clients*	0	4	15

*Frank is not including clients he brought from his previous firm, until pending lawsuits are settled.

Marketing Budget

Value of co-op advertising from wholesalers	$15,000
Out-of-pocket expenses for marketing	$15,000

Other resources:

Part-time intern from local college
Exchanging financial planning services for a web site and online support from a web expert

Advertising in Practice

This section refers to material discussed in Chapter 4.

IG. Determining When Advertising Is Appropriate

As Inez's business grew, she needed to keep the pipeline filled for her sales staff. She decided it was time to advertise the "Women's Planning Group" (WPG). She identified a local women's business web site and a women's association publication that reached a fair percentage of her target audience. Inez wanted the advertising message to convey urgency and address the importance of planning for both individual and business success. Inez hired a client who owned a small advertising agency to write two ads—one offering a free planning session with WPG and the other an invitation to a seminar. Inez assigned one of her staff to work directly with the publications on the ad layouts and deadlines.

Her ads were successful in bringing in new prospects and her team started closing sales. She also started receiving phone calls from ad sales reps at local and regional publications and online sites, which began taking up her valuable time. Since she was also running regular recruiting ads and would need to begin advertising in Spanish when she added Hispanic sales associates, Inez decided to hire the ad agency to handle her account.

RW. Advertising for Corporate Buyers

While Ron doesn't have to worry about consumer advertising, which is handled by the home office, he does offer co-op advertising opportunities to interested brokers. For example, if a broker wishes to offer a seminar to potential business clients about retirement planning for their employees, Ron's company will provide the brokers with all the necessary seminar materials, including ads for their local publications. A local advertising manager at the home office helps the brokers with placement and ensures that any advertising is in compliance with all applicable laws and regulations.

BDM. Local Advertising

As a first tactic, Bonnie-Dee asked the branch managers to prepare a list of local nonprofit community organizations that served wealthy seniors. These included independent living and senior homeowner organizations, recreational and cultural centers (including golf clubs, music groups, and museums), religious organizations, and health-care providers (including hospitals and rehab centers). The branch managers were asked to approach the managers of these organizations to gauge interest in working with ABC Bank on the SAIF initiative.

Organizations that agreed to participate would be prominently featured as co-sponsors in the SAIF advertising. Customized posters were created for each participating site, advertising a series of breakfast meetings and indicating that the bank would be making a donation to the nonprofit organization on behalf of each attendee.

Frank Aldrich, Financial Adviser, Congratulates the XYZ Club on Its 18th Annual Tournament

---

The children who were born when the tournament got its start are now ready for college. Will you be ready for college when your children are? For a no-cost, no-obligation consultation on college funding, retirement planning, or other financial goals, please call me at 215-555-1234 or visit us at www.aldrichfinancial.com.

Organizational partners were given other customized materials, including invitation kits for their members/clients.

FA. A First Ad

Frank's first advertising opportunity arose when the country club asked him to buy a placement in its annual commemorative edition, held in conjunction with its golf tournament. Since Frank was one of the tournament's sponsors, the ad was included in his package. But what should it say?

Frank looked at the previous year's book and saw that most advertisers used their half pages to congratulate the players or the club. But Frank didn't want to waste the opportunity to market his financial advisory business. After all, the people who would see this were his target markets and they would probably keep the book for a long time. Still, he had to be subtle about the message—it shouldn't appear to be too self-serving.

Frank had a friend who wrote copy for catalogues, and she offered to write his ad. What she came up with was appropriate to the occasion but also fit with Frank's objectives of creating awareness of his services as a financial adviser:

The printer who printed the book laid out the ad for Frank according to his guidelines (serif type, black letters on white background). Frank also liked the line "Will you be ready for college when your children are?" so he asked his friend to turn it into an ad for other publications.

Public Relations in Practice

This section refers to material discussed in Chapter 5.

IG. Getting Out the Word About the Women's Planning Group

Inez G. recognized the value of the press after she read an article about financial planning and it quoted a competitor. She believed her competitor was well positioned in the article, and the story provided a lot of good information. Her feeling was confirmed when two days later one of her best clients called to ask if she had seen the story and to question why Inez wasn't quoted.

Inez called her team together and set out to develop a PR action plan that included personally building relationships with reporters and editors. She knew this was critical if she wanted reporters to think of the Women's Planning Group when they needed information on financial planning or a quote from a financial planning expert. One of the insurance companies whose products she represented offered her the use of prewritten, compliance-approved articles on financial planning for women business owners. Her team submitted these articles, with Inez's byline, for placement in local business and general market publications and web sites. The staff posted announcements of each of the WPG's monthly seminars to the company's blog, Facebook and LinkedIn pages, along with a "Financial Planning Tip of the Month." This short, two- or three-sentence piece of financial planning advice included a quote from Inez or one of her agents. It was frequently picked up as filler by the local publications and bloggers.

RW. Institutional PR

Ron took every opportunity to speak to groups of brokers. If the brokers' parent company was having a training program or seminar on financial planning for entrepreneurs, Ron got in touch with the organizers to see if there was a place on the program for him to talk about retirement plans for small business. Ron was also a frequent speaker at professional organizations and wrote a regular column on retirement planning for an online publication read by many of his target brokers. He even helped his clients get publicity—for example, because he knew all the chamber of commerce directors within his territory, he often helped his client brokers get in front of business owners.

BDM. Generating Publicity for the SAIF Program

Continuing to operate on a local level as she had done for her advertising, Bonnie-Dee asked her branch bank managers to provide contact names for media outlets, including newspapers and other publications, radio programs favored by the target market, broadcast and cable television news operations, and online sites. The bank sent a media alert offering an interview with one of the bank's top investment advisers, commenting on how market volatility could affect seniors' income. Press releases and Facebook posts were created for the branches to send out under their own names, announcing the Silver Assets Investment Focus program, with new releases issued for the announcement of each major co-sponsor. As the breakfast series got under way, members of the media were invited to attend and to follow up directly with the investment adviser if they had questions. The bank's central marketing department also prepared a series of articles, to be offered to the media under the investment advisers' byline.

FA. A Public Relations Investment Pays Off

While attending a chamber of commerce luncheon meeting, Frank listened to a speaker discuss the "Power and Importance of Publicity in Building a Practice." He was impressed by what he heard and began to see the value in publicity. His first instinct was to hire the speaker, an independent specialist, to handle his PR. But her price of $900 for a single press release was too steep for Frank's budget.

He did feel that he had picked up a few pointers from the speaker, and Frank began developing his strategy by asking his college intern to research a list of questions.

- What are the media outlets in my area? Specifically, what are the names of community newspapers, business publications, radio stations, broadcast and cable stations, regional magazines, and web sites that target the region? The intern researched the information online and at the library and made follow-up calls. Frank checked out the web sites of the media that he was interested in contacting, and he personally took a look at the programming on the TV and radio outlets that the intern had listed.
- Which editor should I contact? Is there a business editor? Where there was not, Frank's intern called the managing editor and asked her (or her assistant) to whom to address his queries.
- What types of information are most important to the outlet, such as business, lifestyle, politics, social, or general interest? Knowing the editorial focus of the media outlet helped identify stories that were most appropriate to readers.
- What are the deadlines? For daily newspapers, deadlines have little or no flexibility and must be adhered to rigorously.
- What is the outlet's preferred way to receive information (press release, link to a web site)?

Frank then developed a checklist of how he could use publicity to benefit his business:

Serve as a source for quotes as a financial planning expert. From his listening and reading, he compiled a list of reporters who regularly covered financial planning stories. He contacted each of them and asked if they would be interested in doing an interview or needed help with any stories. Although none of them had interest in the interview, they all said they would put Frank into their contact lists. He followed up with a brief e-mail to each, thanking them for their courtesy and including a brief bio and a list of topics on which he was prepared to speak.

A few weeks later, Frank got a call from Jim Sawyer at the *Bucks County Courier*, who was researching a story on a possible change in plan managers for Pennsylvania's 529 Plan. Frank hadn't heard the rumors but offered to check with some people he knew and call Jim back, which he did within the time frame promised. That week's story quoted Frank. The next day, Frank got a call from a reporter at the *Philadelphia Inquirer* who had read the *Bucks County* piece and wanted more information from Frank. Frank was quoted in that story, too. Then Frank read a story in the *Wall Street Journal* and saw that there was an inaccuracy. He posted a comment online citing the correct information. The next day, Frank received e-mails from bloggers and reporters around the country who were seeking information on 529 Plans. Because Frank was ready with quick and accurate responses, he became a source on issues concerning college financing.

Create articles about specific financial topics. Frank called the editors at several local papers and radio stations to find out if they accepted articles on financial planning subjects. One editor at the *Trenton Times* seemed to be interested, but Frank had trouble getting in touch with her to follow up. He decided to write a story anyway, a general piece on college funding. He asked a friend who was a teacher to review the piece before he sent it to make sure it was interesting to a prospective client, easy to read, and grammatically correct. He then e-mailed it to the editor. When he did not hear back from her, he followed up by phone.

She apologized for being difficult to reach, but noted that she was doing two peoples' jobs while her colleague was out on maternity leave. She said she had read the article he had submitted and was interested in running it, but had no budget to pay him. He assured her that it wasn't necessary—the publicity would be his payment. After the first article ran, he got two calls from interested prospects. He also obtained permission to reprint the article and e-mailed it to all his current clients, along with a personalized cover note saying "In case you missed this" and giving his name and phone number. He received two additional calls from that e-mailing and one from a prospect who had been referred to Frank from a current client who was very impressed with his article. By that point, Frank felt that he was beginning to receive a good return on the value of the considerable time he had invested in his PR initiatives.

Find out about doing a regular financial advice column for the local paper, radio or online outlet (i.e., planning tips, retirement information, college funding, etc.). Eventually, the *Trenton Times* editor asked him to write a regular column for the paper's web site on financial planning, which became a regular source of new prospects.

Other ideas for Frank's promotions:

- Post a blog containing all his college-planning articles and send a link to clients and prospects.
- Organize a seminar about college financing at a high school or grammar school.
- Send out a press release about his seminars beforehand.
- Send out an article on the same topic after each presentation.
- Give attendees a printed copy of the article.

Sponsorship in Practice

This section refers to material discussed in Chapter 6.

IG. Fitting Sponsorships to Brand Image

Inez was approached by one of her daughter's coaches about sponsoring the girls' soccer team. Inez was delighted to accept—not only for her daughter's sake, but also because the sponsorship meshed with her business objectives. The association of The Women's Planning Group with girls' sports was exactly on message: encouraging women to be independent, strong, and able to compete. For less than a thousand dollars, The Women's Planning Group would be on T-shirts worn by fifteen 10-year-old girls, on signage at the games, and in an acknowledgment in the sports annual published by the school.

In addition to enhancing the brand image of her company, this modest investment helped get her company's name out to parents, teachers, coaches, and spectators. It also demonstrated the company's commitment to the community, thus creating goodwill.

RW. Corporate Sponsorships and Personal Charitable Activities

Although the home office made the decisions about national sponsorships at the corporate level, Ron requested that National Mutual Fund Company put its name behind some local events as well. Since many of Ron's client brokers met with their small-business customers on the golf course, Ron asked NMFC to participate as a sponsor of several local golf tournaments, where he entertained his clients and their clients at a hospitality suite. He also asked his firm to contribute to some charity fund drives, especially those that were also underwritten by his client organizations.

As an African American, Ron was particularly supportive of black business owners and was active in fund-raising and mentoring activities for local chapters of scholarship programs for minority business students. Although these activities were personal, they established Ron as a "player" in his community, and he received honors from several organizations. The contacts he built among both black and white community leaders were enormously helpful in building his career success.

BDM. The Value of Cause Marketing

When one of Bonnie-Dee's branch managers approached the Boca Raton Museum of Art about the SAIF seminar program, she was met with a counterproposal. The museum would be happy to co-sponsor the bank's Silver Assets Investment Focus program to its members (most of whom were in the target age/wealth range) in exchange for ABC Bank's sponsoring an exhibit at the museum. The branch manager passed the request on to Bonnie-Dee, who discussed it with her management. The community affairs department of the bank became involved in the discussions, which ended with the bank's agreeing to sponsor an exhibit featuring pre–twentieth-century architecture in the region. One of the most prominent items on display was to be a cast model of the first bank in South Florida.

ABC Bank not only agreed to pay for the exhibit and its related advertising and publicity costs, it also agreed to pay for the creation of the scaled down model, using original architectural drawings. Because the bank licensed the rights to the model, they were able to use depictions of it as the focal point for their advertising—and to commission a company to create small, piggy-bank size versions to distribute to SAIF participants.

The bank was very pleased by the synergy created between the SAIF program and the museum, which resulted in publicity and goodwill far beyond what the SAIF program itself would have generated.

FA. Weighing Costs and Benefits

Frank A. had his first taste of what it is like to be an event sponsor when he agreed to become a silver sponsor of a golf outing to support a local college scholarship fund.

Frank identified this as an effective opportunity to meet his business objectives for several reasons:

- His practice specializes in college funding, so association with a college scholarship was a natural match.
- His target client base included plenty of golfers. Since the club holding the outing was not Frank's home club, he would get an opportunity to meet new prospects.
- Because players included celebrity guests (some Philadelphia Eagles and 76ers players, among others), the outing was likely to be featured in local newspapers and newscasts. This coverage would enable Frank to extend his name involvement through public relations.

For Frank's $2,500 contribution, he was entitled to a foursome of golf, signage at the first tee, his company name on all communications, a company banner at the awards dinner, an ad in the program book, and recognition from the podium for his contribution and support. Also, he had the opportunity to contribute an item to the gift bag each player would receive.

This sounded great and he thought well worth his $2,500 investment. Like many sponsors, what Frank didn't realize was that his $2,500 investment was just the start. He also needed to activate his sponsorship, and he didn't have much time. He went to a print shop to have the signage for the first tee and banner created, which cost $600. He also decided he would donate a sleeve of golf balls for each gift bag. They had to have his logo on them, so he had to buy twenty boxes of logoed golf balls at a cost of $26 a box, which came to another $520. He also had to figure another $200 for lunch and drinks for the members of his foursome. So his initial $2,500 investment was now more than $3,800. Frank was finding out the hard way that activation costs generally add between 50 percent and 150 percent to the expense of the sponsorship itself.

Frank was still satisfied that he made the right decision, but now he realized that the sponsorship fee was just the start of the time and money that made an event a success. An additional investment was needed to convey the fact of his sponsorship to his target markets and make the event memorable for guests.

Interactive Marketing in Practice

This section refers to material discussed in Chapter 7.

IG. Identifying the Need for Interactive Marketing

Inez and her team had built up a network of contacts through online and offline research, including articles about new women-owned businesses, chamber of commerce and National Association of Women Business Owners (NAWBO) membership lists, seminar attendees, word-of-mouth, LinkedIn and Facebook groups, and other networking activities. To stay front of mind to these potential clients, Inez began by joining online forums and networks, where she or her staff posted answers to questions or posed their own and actively sought out new contacts. They decided to publish a monthly e-newsletter and sent links to her contact lists. A decision was made not to try to sell through the e-mailing, but rather to use the newsletter to develop sales leads. Each newsletter included an article of interest to the woman business owner, with a cover letter from Inez emphasizing the importance of financial planning for business owners.

In addition to the e-mails, where the team had phone numbers, they began a phone campaign. Because their prospects were businesses, not consumers, "do not call" regulations did not apply. The team made phone calls from 8 a.m. to 10 a.m., introducing themselves to prospects and setting up appointments to meet. Where possible, coffee meetings were arranged, where a Women's Planning Group team member would meet the prospect for a cup of coffee before the start of the business day. These e-mailings and calls resulted in a continual stream of new prospects.

RW. Using Purchased Lists for Additional Leads

Since no one in Ron's territory was covering independent brokers and financial advisers, Ron convinced the home office that it would be worthwhile to do a test mailing of unaffiliated brokers for new business proposals.

Ron told the home office direct mail experts what he was looking for—independent brokers within his sales territory who specialized in small- to medium-sized business clients. They came up with a list of 750 names. They prepared a letter in Ron W.'s name, which they sent in a plain #10 business envelope with no message on the outer envelope, mailed first class. The envelope also contained a brochure that NMFC had in stock, titled, "Increasing Your Business with Business Retirement Plans."

The call to action was a request for more information. Recipients could mail back a postage-paid card, addressed to Ron W., or they could e-mail or call him directly—his contact information was included in the letter. Altogether, the mailing cost a little over $1,500. From the 750 names mailed, Ron got 10 responses, a rate of a little over 1 percent. He eventually converted four of the independent brokers into clients worth hundreds of thousands of dollars. So, clearly, the effort was profitable. Next time, Ron planned to roll out similar mailings in waves of 50 and follow up with a personal phone call.

BDM. Interactive Marketing for the SAIF Program

As noted in the "Advertising in Practice" section, the branches asked their co-sponsors for lists of potential invitees. The branches then filled in the names on preprinted invitations, which included the name of the co-sponsor. In some cases, the sponsor preferred not to give the branch its membership list and filled in the invitations themselves.

Some branches sought to supplement the co-sponsors' lists with purchased lists. Bonnie-Dee gave permission for each branch to spend up to $1,500 for purchase of names meeting certain requirements: within a given zip code, age 60 and above, investable assets of $250,000 or more.

Each branch was to sponsor one breakfast every three months. By inviting 300 attendees to each breakfast, they hoped to draw at least 50 people (including guests). Although the projected response rate was ambitious, the direct mail professionals at the bank thought it was achievable, for several reasons. The target market of retired people had time on their hands. They would be drawn by the subject ("Successful investing tactics in a volatile market"); by the food catered by local restaurants known for their ample Southern breakfasts; and by the chance to be with other retirees, especially those who belonged to similar community organizations. Since they were invited to bring as many guests as they liked, even a 10 percent response rate could result in more than 50 attendees, if each brought just one guest. Current clients of the bank were invited by phone and encouraged to bring their own guests. To ensure a good turnout of those who had responded, branch personnel called with a reminder a few days before the breakfast. The response rate exceeded expectations, and in some cases invitees had to be waitlisted for a future breakfast.

FA. Making Interactive Marketing Effective

Like Inez, Frank began his networking with a search of web sites, LinkedIn, and Facebook groups devoted to his local community. His college intern helped him make Facebook and LinkedIn requests to all his contacts and to online prospects who lived in the community and met the demographic target.

He also had membership lists of his country club and his church. There were about 700 households in total. The first thing Frank did was go through both lists, removing any name that appeared on both lists. He also created a separate list of the 120 families he knew well enough to contact in person.

Frank decided to send an e-mail to his online network and a letter to the 450 people in his directory database, in conjunction with a talk he was giving on college funding at a local library.

When Frank worked for the brokerage, they provided materials to help him prospect—sales letters, seminar kits, ads for local publications. Now he would have to develop some of these materials on his own.

Frank had a friend who was a professional catalogue copywriter who offered to help create his mailing package. With Frank's help, the writer composed two different letters. To the 450 people who shared his country club or church affiliation, he wrote a very personal letter, which began as follows:

> Dear first name, last name,
>   As a fellow member of (name of club/church), we have probably shared a locker room (or church pew). Perhaps your children play with my children, Dan (10) and Ella (6). If we haven't met yet, I hope we will soon, because we have a lot of common interests and hopes for the future.
>   One of my hopes for the future is that my children will be able to attend the college of their choice, regardless of cost . . .

For the e-mail, he wrote a little less intimately, but still personally. The subject head was: "College Funding 101." It began

> As a parent of a 10 and a 6 year old, I know that paying for college is a major concern. While my children are still young, I've begun to put money away for college because I know that the earlier I start, the more time the funds will be able to grow.

In both letters, Frank went on to explain who he is and what his credentials are. For the letter mailing, he included an article he had written about college financing. For the e-mailing, Frank prominently linked to an article he had posted with the title "College Funding 101."

He closed with an invitation to attend his presentation on saving for college at the local library. If the person couldn't make it, he'd be happy to set up an appointment to meet with him or her personally. Frank included his phone number and e-mail address.

For those who requested a personal meeting or more information, Frank followed up with a call. In addition, a few days before the seminar, Frank followed up with a phone reminder to everyone who said they would attend. He then called all 30 people who had attended the seminar within the following week to set up follow-up meetings.

Social Media in Practice

This section refers to material discussed in Chapter 8.

IG. Using Social Media

As noted earlier, Inez's group established a monthly e-newsletter with articles of interest to women business owners. They also created a blog, posting at least once a week about articles they had read or conversations that could stimulate discussion. They interviewed clients about how they were growing their business and the challenges they faced. Comments on the blog became more frequent and Inez saw that Chicago-area women business owners were beginning to use the blog site as a network for issues of concern. She decided to set up a separate LinkedIn group and a Twitter feed for her clients and others who were interested in sharing their experiences and made sure that the links were included whenever she or any of her staff posted to their groups.

RW. Networking with Sales Executives

NMFC had a web site for its broker clients that included not just account information but a variety of sales tools, including customizable proposals, pricing and commission information, and "what-if" scenarios for multiple plan types. Ron convinced the home office to add a sales-skills-building computer game, which brokers could play with each other. Through tracking statistics, Ron saw that the game was getting a lot of hits and he asked the home office to create a downloadable app of the game for smartphones and tablets. The game has become quite popular and it has raised awareness of NMFC among his broker clients. It has also given him a natural lead-in when he is meeting with new clients.

BDM. Using Social Media for Promoting SAIF

Bonnie-Dee did not initially think social media were a useful adjunct to the Silver Assets Investment Focus marketing program, because she thought most seniors did not network online. But ABC Bank's head of interactive marketing soon set her straight— over 42 percent of seniors nationwide used social networking to keep in touch with family and friends, hunt for people from their past, and seek answers to questions.

Facebook pages went up with information about SAIF and the calendar of breakfast seminars. Co-sponsors were also asked to put up information on their Facebook pages. The bank got in touch with networks visited by seniors in south Florida to exchange links and provide content of value.

FA. Multiple Online Applications

For the first year, Frank used social media primarily to gather and disseminate information. He found useful blogs and sites that he checked regularly, to keep up with new developments in his field, to check in with wholesalers to see what programs he might participate in, as background for the articles he wrote and to comment. He regularly communicated with his clients by e-mail reminding them of tax deadlines, setting up appointments, and keeping them apprised of changes that affected their portfolios. He also posted each article he wrote to his web site and e-mailed them to clients and prospects who had given permission.

Frank's intern researched exchanging links between Frank's site and other web sites, blogs, and groups concerned with college funding issues. Using keywords such as "529 Plan and Pennsylvania" for search engine optimization, the intern helped make sure Frank's articles would come up on searches.

Frank started his own blog and invited site visitors to sign up for an e-mail alert. He got sign-ups through the purchase of keyword ads. He also began accepting ads on his blog. The revenues were small but the highly targeted ads covered a part-time salary for his college intern.

Personal Selling in Practice

This section refers to material discussed in Chapter 9.

IG. Leveraging Financial Resources through Co-Op

Inez G. wanted to increase her marketing spending, but she found it difficult to budget enough to cover all the activities she had planned. While attending a monthly meeting, she learned that the home office was launching a co-op program that would pay for up to two-thirds of her marketing expenses depending on the target market and the anticipated outcome. Inez had identified two local charities her group wanted to support as Platinum-level sponsors. In return she would receive the organization's mailing list, have an opportunity to address attendees during the opening session, and have WPG signage throughout the event. Based on the exposure WPG would receive, the home office agreed to fund 60 percent of the sponsorship event.

RW. Changes in a Broker-Wire House Relationship Benefit a Wholesaler

Along with instituting new producer productivity software, the wire houses that Ron worked with were changing the nature of production. Clients were being segmented by asset size, and smaller accounts were being transferred to phone reps. Top producers were expected to handle only accounts with assets of $500,000 or more.

This change actually benefited Ron, whose target market was only the top producers and only those who handled small-business retirement plans. The fact that the phone reps were now segregated from customers did not matter, since Ron did not do business with them. And by giving up some of their smaller accounts, the top reps had more time to develop the small- and medium-sized business customers that bought Ron's retirement product. Therefore, Ron decided to put even more effort into helping his A-level brokers increase the size of their own books of business.

BDM. Personal Selling at the SAIF Seminars

Bonnie-Dee worked with her branch managers and their staffs to ensure that each Silver Assets Investment Focus seminar had sufficient coverage. For 50 guests, there needed to be at least five branch sales staff available (including the branch manager and Bonnie-Dee or a member of her staff). One was seated at each table of 10. The responsibilities of the sales staff were to chat with the guests, to provide materials before the presentation began, and to answer any questions raised after the presentation. The salesperson also gave each guest his or her gift—the miniature bank, boxed and hand-wrapped, with a personalized card from the investment specialist. The salesperson was assigned to work with the investment specialist to follow up with each guest. Bonnie-Dee developed sales contests at both the branch and the individual level to further motivate all the branch staff, including the tellers.

FA. Uses of Co-Op Marketing Materials

Frank had been sticking closely to his marketing plan and he was pleased with the results to date. However, he also realized that he was spending much more than he initially planned or budgeted. As a way to offset some of his marketing costs, Frank looked into a co-op program offered to independent advisers by one of the wholesalers he worked with.

Because this company wanted to grow sales by 20 percent over the next 12 months, it would match, on a 50/50 basis, spending to promote its 529 Plan for education funding. All Frank had to do was submit an application and have it approved.

Since Frank already conducted six seminars a year on college funding, the 50 percent match enabled him to either hold twice as many seminars or continue as planned at half the cost.

Trade Shows and Seminars in Practice

This section refers to material discussed in Chapter 10.

IG. Reaching Decisionmakers through Trade Shows

The Women's Planning Group had exhibited at a handful of trade shows over the past five years, with mixed results. But when Inez learned that the National Association of Women Business Owners was going to hold its national meeting in Chicago, she immediately signed up to exhibit. Here was an opportunity to speak directly with her target audience in an environment that was conducive to information sharing. Further, Inez contacted the national NAWBO headquarters to discuss how she could best leverage her exhibit and to determine the availability of attendee lists for mailings prior to the meeting. She asked about speaking opportunities for herself and her team, and explored hosting an on-site reception for local NAWBO attendees.

RW. Using Seminars to Help Clients Build Their Business

National Mutual Fund Company offered a number of programs for top brokers who sold large amounts of the company's retirement product. These were designed to reward the brokers and to help them continue to build their business. Twice a year, selected brokers were invited to a resort, where they heard from big-name speakers, participated in business seminars, and were wined and dined by NMFC executives. Ron, of course, participated in these events with his clients. In addition, Ron held his own regional events, at local hotels and restaurants, for those brokers who did not qualify for the national events or who chose not to attend. He also brought in speakers, provided by NMFC, and set up seminars and courses designed to give brokers all the tools they needed to expand their small-business retirement assets.

BDM. The SAIF Seminar

Preparations began eight weeks before the date of each SAIF breakfast seminar. All branch staff were involved—hand writing invitations, making follow-up calls, making arrangements with the hotel and caterer, coordinating with the co-sponsor. Each branch received a checklist, outlining every step from "day −30" to "day +60," including timing of reminder calls ("day −5") and follow-up calls (by "day +3," "day +30," "day +60").

Although the breakfast seminars went smoothly for the most part, one last minute glitch nearly sank the efforts of a Miami branch, which had a synagogue as co-sponsor. Nobody had thought to tell the caterer—who specialized in traditional Southern breakfasts with sausages and bacon—that the group required kosher food. The branch manager saved the day by calling around until she found a kosher restaurant that could accommodate the group at short notice.

Overall, the breakfasts were successful. Not only did sales of investment products soar, but ABC Bank received favorable publicity. Although the bank's contributions to its community co-sponsors totaled in the tens of thousands of dollars, the publicity and goodwill generated were worth millions.

FA. Exhibiting at a Trade Show

While attending a chamber of commerce meeting, Frank learned that in two months the local chapter of the American Bar Association would be holding a two-day conference and expo for its members at a nearby hotel. A limited number of exhibit booths would also be made available to local businesses. Frank immediately considered the possibilities. "This," he thought, "would provide an opportunity to get to know a large number of local attorneys." As a financial planner, Frank was always looking to develop business alliances and get referrals.

As soon as he returned to his office, he called the local chapter of the ABA to reserve a booth and determine where in the exhibit hall it would be located. Frank was pleased with the spot and paid for the exhibit space with his credit card. While he was on the phone, he asked the conference coordinator whether there was an opportunity for outside speakers or seminars. He learned that the speakers would all be ABA members and the ABA had booked all of the hotel's conference rooms for its own use. He did ask for, and was told he would receive, a list of all the attendees approximately three to four weeks before the conference began.

Although disappointed, Frank realized that he would never have been able to work a tradeshow and conduct a seminar at the same time. He saw that he was being overly ambitious. He just didn't have the time or staff to exploit both opportunities. He did decide, however, to print invitations to one of his upcoming seminars and make these available to attendees at the show. Frank began developing his to-do list, which included:

- Purchase small logoed giveaway items
- Call some attorney friends to discuss the conference and possible opportunities
- Prepare an invitation for attendees to stop by his booth and enter a raffle
- Purchase raffle gift ($150 gift certificate to one of the newest and hottest restaurants)
- Create a special invitation to his next seminar on college funding

Once he completed his list, he considered how he would arrange his booth space. He decided that he wanted his 8 foot × 10 foot space to be as inviting as possible, so he would have only one table in the back of the booth with information. He had a tabletop display, highlighting his services, which he would set up on the display table. He also would rent some comfortable chairs so attendees could sit down while Frank spoke with them and so that other attendees could just stop by and take a break. He might even rent a coffee urn and serve coffee all day long, he thought.

Relationship Marketing in Practice

This section refers to material discussed in Chapter 11.

IG. Creating Loyalty among the Best Clients

Inez G. knew she needed a process for communicating with her most valued customers and prospects on a regular basis. The firm's customer database was segmented by value of the account and type of product. Prospects were ranked on a subjective scale of 1 to 10 based on the agent's estimation of the individual's likelihood to buy and amount of prospective business.

Everyone on the database list received the group's online newsletter. The top 20 percent of customers and prospects received a phone call at least once a quarter. The next 30 percent were called twice a year. The bottom 50 percent received an annual "financial check-up" letter and a phone call.

RW. Building Relationships with Institutional Clients

Ron W. devoted half his marketing budget to relationship-building—that is, efforts to retain his broker clients, increase the amount of business they did with NMFC, and generate referrals to other brokers. Ron used a number of methods to maintain the relationships, such as his and NMFC's seminar program and web site. NMFC also created an online newsletter full of useful selling information, special studies of the small-business market conducted on behalf of their clients, and other information that they continually made available to top brokers. Ron supplemented the home office material with his own online publication, which featured sales successes. For each brokerage firm, he produced a bimonthly e-letter that featured a broker who had made a large or complex sale, outlining the tactics the broker had used to get the business. Other brokers found this information helped them to make their own sales.

The biggest portion of Ron's retention marketing budget went to day-to-day activities, such as inviting client brokers and their clients to a sports event or dinner at a top restaurant. Ron had purchased corporate boxes for local sports teams, and if he wasn't available to meet and greet his guests, he'd pass along the tickets anyway. Ron wrote personal notes for special occasions, such as weddings, birth of children, and holidays.

BDM. Keeping SAIF Clients Happy

Bringing in so much new investment business with the SAIF breakfasts was a coup for Bonnie-Dee, but she knew that it was only the first step. Now she had to plan ways to keep her new clients happy in order to retain their business, get additional business from them, and get additional referrals.

With her senior managers' approval, Bonnie-Dee contracted with an investment education firm to create a special program for SAIF members. Called SAIF Harbor, the program consisted of several parts:

- A regular monthly late afternoon get-together for all SAIF members at a local yacht club. Each get-together featured an ABC Bank investment specialist speaker along with tea and sandwiches. The cost was low (the yacht club agreed to donate the space in the hopes of generating party business from the SAIF members), and those who attended (about 5 to 10 percent of members on any given day) were delighted to have an opportunity to meet one another.
- A regular newsletter called The SAIF Voyager, distributed quarterly by mail and monthly by e-mail. The newsletters, naturally, were designed with a nautical theme. One regular feature, called "The Captain's Table," offered a summary of the speaker's remarks at the monthly get-togethers, along with photos of those in attendance. Another, "Shipboard Chatter," offered news about members. Merchants were solicited to offer discounts to members, and these were publicized in the "Ship's Gift Shop." There was also information about ABC Bank—news releases, new products, and a regular economic insights column edited from white papers prepared by ABC Bank's chief economist. There was even a bridge column (called, naturally, "On the Bridge"), written on a voluntary basis by two SAIF members.
- Regular follow-up contacts. The investment adviser arranged a regular schedule of follow-ups with the client. Most clients chose a monthly call, which generally lasted between 15 and 30 minutes. These calls were not only a big hit with SAIF members but resulted in significant new assets transferred to ABC Bank, along with a steady supply of referral business.

FA. Building a Loyal Individual Client Base

At the end of his first year, Frank examined his client base and prospect list, and divided it into two groups:

1. A list. These were both clients and prospects who were likely to be worth more than $20,000 a year in fee business.
2. B list. Those worth less than $20,000 per year.

Here is what Frank decided he should do for his A group:

- Personally handle all questions, returning any messages within 12 hours
- Call them at least once every two months
- Send them articles of interest based on the profiles Frank created for each client.

- Ask each client to link on Facebook and LinkedIn. Set a Google Alerts for each client. Set an automated alert from his profile software to notify him of birthdays, anniversaries, and other triggers.
- Invite clients to the annual charity golf outing which Frank co-sponsors.
- If the clients were not golfers, invite them with their families to an amusement park for a charity outing which he also co-sponsors.

For the remaining clients, Frank made sure that he or his assistant returned calls within 24 hours and that one of them called the client at least once every three months. In addition, he would:

- On regular calls, while inquiring about any changes/questions, ask the client for referrals to others who might be interested in Frank's services
- Immediately send a thank-you note after any referral
- If a referral was significant ("A level"), invite both referrer and new client to lunch at the club
- Send a personalized e-mail or printed card if he learns about a major event in the client's life
- Keep an online, up-to-date record of all important client information, including names, ages, and birth dates of spouse and children, who referred them, whether this client has given any referrals, and so on.
- Send a personalized holiday greeting card (hand-signed by Frank or his assistant)

Conclusion

Using basic marketing principles can improve the efficiency and profitability of every sales effort. The authors look forward to engaging with those in the field through our web site, http://www.fsmhandbook.com., where you will find additional examples, frequently asked questions, and more.

About the Authors

Evelyn Ehrlich, Ph.D

Evelyn Ehrlich, President of EC Communications, has been a specialist in financial marketing strategy and communications since 1982, for such clients as AXA Equitable, BNY Mellon, JPMorgan Chase, Merrill Lynch, and many other financial institutions across industry sub-segments.

Dr. Ehrlich has a bachelor of arts from Barnard College, a master of science from Columbia University, and received her doctorate from New York University. She began her career as a college professor and consultant, and currently teaches Financial Services Marketing at New York University with Duke Fanelli.

Dr. Ehrlich is the author of *Cinema of Paradox: French Filmmaking under the Occupation* (Columbia UP, 1985), and is co-editor of *The Practical Marketing Handbook Series for Community Bankers,* published by Americas Community Bankers (now part of the American Bankers Association).

Duke Fanelli

Louis "Duke" Fanelli has more than 25 years' experience in marketing and financial services. He is currently Senior Vice President, Marketing and Communication for the ANA (Association of National Advertisers) the leading association for client-side marketers. Prior to joining ANA in 2010, he served as the Chief Marketing Officer for Edelman Financial Services, Fairfax, Virginia, a leading independent advisory firm specializing in asset and wealth management.

Duke developed his communication and marketing expertise across both retail banking and insurance, leading strategic and tactical program development. Earlier, he was a Vice President of Marketing for AXA Equitable Life Insurance Co., New York, where he managed the company's field-marketing program as well as its multicultural and sponsorship marketing activities. Prior to joining AXA, he spent nearly 15 years in various communication, marketing, and business leadership positions at Chase Bank. He began his career as a journalist, later moving into account management for a New York City-based public relations firm and entered the financial services industry as a communication specialist.

Index

Printed and bound by CPI Group (UK) Ltd, Croydon, CR0 4YY

16/04/2025

14658463-0003